Bold As Lions

The Future Belongs To The Righteous

BRIAN GIBBS

BOLD AS LIONS
The Future Belongs To The Righteous
Copyright © 2017, By Brian Gibbs
Published in The United States Of America

Scripture quotations taken from the New King James Version.
Copyright © 1982 by Thomas Nelson, Inc.
Used by permission. All rights reserved.

Scripture quotations taken from the Amplified® Bible (AMP)
Copyright © 2015 Used by permission. All rights reserved.

Scripture quotations taken from the New Living Translation
Copyright ©1996, 2004, 2007, 2013, 2015
Used by permission. All rights reserved.

Scripture quotations marked The Bible: James Moffatt Translation
Copyright © 1922, 1924, 1925, 1926, 1935 Harper Collins San Francisco,
Copyright © 1950, 1952, 1953, 1954 James A. R. Moffatt.
Used by permission. All rights reserved.

No part of this publication may be reproduced, stored in a retrieval system
or transmitted in any form or by any other means – electronic, mechanical,
photocopying, recording or otherwise – without the prior written permission
of the publisher and copyright owners.

Published by Brian & Bren Gibbs
Light The Fire Ministries
P.O. Box 51586
Sarasota, Florida 34232

Light The Fire Ministries
Igniting Revival, Equipping Leaders & Reforming America
www.lightthefireministries.org

Bold As Lions
The Future Belongs To The Righteous

1
Victorious Lion
Inheritance of Glory

2
Courage
In An Age Of Compromise & Conformity

3
Integrity & Honor
The Call of the Noble

4
Prevailing Church
The Ekklesia of Glory & Victory

5
Stewarding The Future
His Manifest Presence

6
Invading The Darkness
An Epic Commission

7
Champions
The Rise & Roar Of Sons & Daughters

8
Leadership
The Pathway To Triumph

Dedication
To My Lord & Savior — Jesus Christ.
To every courageous lion-heart who treasures
His heart and answers His calling.
Be Bold. Be Strong. Be Wise.

Special Thanks
My Greatest Joy & Love of My Life.
Bren, Josiah & Victoria
I love you with all my heart.

Light The Fire Ministries — Friends & Partners
Victory: A Church Of His Presence
Sarasota, Florida

Bren Gibbs, Jonna Broadway
Nate Estelle & Steve Hansen

Chapter 1

VICTORIOUS LION
Inheritance of Glory

The sunlight came cracking through the morning darkness to shine upon the hills of Jerusalem. It was a day like no other day in human history. The stone had been rolled away. Inside an empty, borrowed tomb laid the grave cloths and facial cloth of the Lamb of God that had been brutally slain for the salvation of the world. This was the day of Resurrection. The Lamb was now the triumphant and victorious Lion. The Son of God, the Son of Abraham, the Son of David — The Lord Jesus Christ was risen — defeating death, conquering hell and alive forever more.

It was a quiet and dark morning as Mary had made her way early to a garden to discover the marvel of an empty tomb. While Peter and John investigated the linens, Mary wept, overwhelmed and perplexed, assuming that Jesus body had been taken away in secret. Suddenly, without warning, two angels appeared at the tomb. They asked her why she was weeping. As she tried to explain her dilemma, the Lion approached her from behind. He asked her why she was weeping and who did she come seeking? As she considered Him to be perhaps the gardener, she begged to know where His body was taken. Then Jesus said to her, "Mary," and suddenly the mystery was no longer hidden from her eyes and heart. It was The Lord Jesus!

The instructions that Jesus gave her next were electrifying. He told Mary not to cling to him because he had another special assignment that morning — in heaven. He told her that He had not yet ascended to His Father, but to go and tell the others that He was ascending to His Father and their Father, to His God and their God (see John 20). The garden was to become a launching pad for our High Priest to transcend time and space.

The Apostle Paul writes in Hebrew that our High Priest, Jesus Christ, ascended to God Almighty, soaring and passing through the heavens. Upon His glorious arrival, all of heaven celebrated the Only Begotten, the Incorruptible One, as He walked through the courts of heaven into the Holy of Holies, the very throne of God, to offer once and for all His own blood upon the mercy seat to establish and invoke a new and living covenant of grace. This was the Day of Atonement. This was a day like no other day, from eternity past, until the appearing of the Victorious Lion.

He was forever the Lamb slain from the foundation of the world — given to redeem and save — now crucified, buried, resurrected, ascended, glorified to become our Mediator and King of Love!

King Of Kings & Lord Of Lords

The roar of endless praise and wild celebration shook the heavens as the radiant King stood in triumph. His eyes burning with fire, His countenance strong and fierce. His presence and form shined more brilliant than the sun. Ecstatic joy and laughter filled all creation. Saints, angels and creatures bowed low in wonder and honor. The angels gasped as they looked upon His hands and feet. All they could say was, "Holy, Holy, Holy."

Flashes of lightning and breaking rolls of thunder illuminated the atmosphere. All around the throne, new sounds and songs of majesty and dominion burst into colors, fire and dance ascribing victory, power and supremacy unto The Risen Lion.

His sacred mission was fulfilled. His violent scourging, whipping post and cross now behind Him. His Father's dream was accomplished for heaven and earth to be one. The veil of heaven opened. Redemption sealed eternally in blood. The Perfection of sacrifice received by fire. The curse and power of sin destroyed. The keys of death and hell secured. The warfare ended. The enemy defeated. The Righteous Son now glorified.

Who could have fathomed such an all-consuming victory? Who could have dreamed such a dream? Who could have orchestrated such a masterpiece? A mystery and secret from eternity past was now realized and unveiled for the ages to come.

Messiah, Lord & Christ
Isaiah 53

"Who has believed our report? And to whom has the arm of the Lord been revealed? For He shall grow up before Him as a tender plant, and as a root out of dry ground. He has no form or comeliness; And when we see Him, there is no beauty that we should desire Him.

He is despised and rejected by men, a Man of sorrows and acquainted with grief. And we hid, as it were, our faces from Him; He was despised, and we did not esteem Him. Surely He has borne our griefs and carried our sorrows; yet we esteemed Him stricken, smitten by God, and afflicted.

But He was wounded for our transgressions, He was bruised for our iniquities; the chastisement for our peace was upon Him, and by His stripes we are healed. All we like sheep have gone astray; we have turned, every one, to his own way; and the Lord has laid on Him the iniquity of us all.

He was oppressed and He was afflicted, yet He opened not His mouth; He was led as a lamb to the slaughter, and as a sheep before its shearers is silent, so He opened not His mouth. He was taken from prison and from judgment, And who will declare His generation?

For He was cut off from the land of the living; for the transgressions of My people He was stricken. And they made His grave with the wicked — but with the rich at His death, Because He had done no violence, Nor was any deceit in His mouth.

Yet it pleased the Lord to bruise Him; He has put Him to grief. When You make His soul an offering for sin, He shall see His seed, He shall prolong His days, and the pleasure of the Lord shall prosper in His hand. He shall see the labor of His soul, and be satisfied.

By His knowledge My righteous Servant shall justify many, for He shall bear their iniquities. Therefore I will divide Him a portion with the great, and He shall divide the spoil with the strong, Because He poured out His soul unto death, and He was numbered with the transgressors, and He bore the sin of many, and made intercession for the transgressors."

BOLD AS LIONS

The Gospel Of Glory
"I have been entrusted with the gospel of the glory of the blessed God."
1 Timothy 1:11

This breathtaking mystery and paradox of the glory of God is the greatest Gift of all. This gospel that has been revealed to us is filled with glory and wonder. Paul calls it the *"the gospel of glory."* In 2 Corinthians we see this phrase *"the gospel of the glory of Christ, who is the image of God." "For it is God who commanded light to shine out of darkness, who has shone in our hearts to give the light of the knowledge of the glory of God in the face of Jesus Christ"* (2 Corinthians 4:4,6).

The glory of God is revealed in the magnificence of the death and resurrection of our Lord Jesus Christ. The gospel of glory is not only an astonishment to angels and creatures, but it is the most profound mystery by God the Father to us. Christ is the Glory and the face of God (see Ephesians 1:6). Paul continues this focus on the gospel of glory to Timothy, ascribing to the Lord, *"To the King of the ages, immortal, invisible, the only God, be honor and glory forever and ever. Amen"* (1 Timothy 1:17).

God's glory in Christ is what has rescued, ransomed and redeemed us. It is His glory that has sealed us as sons and daughters and is the keeping power of God. *"Now to him who is able to keep you from stumbling and to present you blameless before the presence of his glory with great joy, to the only God, our Savior, through Jesus Christ our Lord, be glory, majesty, dominion, and authority, before all time and now and forever. Amen"* (Jude 1:24,25).

The Gospel of Christ is glorious. Religion is the miserable and failed attempt of man trying to reach God. In religion, man tries to cling and hang onto God, but the good news is, in Christ, God clings to man in covenant and unbreakable love. By His own blood, He freed us from our sins. It was His dream to rescue us from our enemies. It was His dream to break our chains of iniquity and infirmities. He was stricken, smitten and afflicted by God Almighty. Jesus was wounded for our transgressions and was bruised for our iniquities. This is not a love of this world. This is a love that knows no limitations — a love far stronger and superior than death.

The Father's dream was that in Christ, who is the glory of God, He would kill the power of sin and death through His cross. The Lord

VICTORIOUS LION

knew no sin, and yet He willingly became sin and a curse for us. In this act of complete love and obedience, He bought our freedom. Paul writes, *"For He made Him who knew no sin to be sin for us, that we might become the righteousness of God in Him"* (2 Corinthians 5:21). This is the gospel of glory - The Light that shines forth into the darkness and darkness cannot comprehend it (see John 1:5). *"He has delivered us from the power of darkness and conveyed us into the kingdom of the Son of His love, in whom we have redemption through His blood, the forgiveness of sins"* (Colossians 1:13,14).

Victory & Ascension
"The earth will be filled with the knowledge of the glory of the Lord as the waters cover the sea."
Habakkuk 2:14

Religion continues to paint a picture of man's utter hopelessness to get to God. I want to tell you that God's plan is so beautiful and masterful that He's left nothing to chance to totally redeem and secure us as His own children. God knew that you and I could never pay the debt we owed. The sacrifice and offering for sin could only be paid by, The Righteous Son.

This dream of total victory would be accomplished in Jesus. Paul writes, when He was crucified, we were crucified with Him. When He was buried, we too were buried with Him. When God raised His Son from the dead, we too were raised. When Jesus ascended to the Father, we ascended and were seated in heavenly places in Christ. This is the Gospel of glory (Galatians 2:20, Romans 6:4, Colossians 2:12, Colossians 3:1, Ephesians 1:20- 2:10).

You've heard the old statement, "killing two birds with one stone." God killed the power and curse of sin for all humanity with one brutal and horrific cross, one perfect sacrifice, one spotless Lamb. Without the cross, we have no freedom, nothing but eternal damnation and the penalty of our sins. But God, who is rich in mercy and love, offered His only begotten Son.

"For God so loved the world that He gave His only begotten Son, that whoever believes in Him should not perish but have everlasting life. For God did not send His Son into the

BOLD AS LIONS

world to condemn the world, but that the world through Him might be saved.
John 3:16 & 17

These words above are perhaps the most beautiful and treasured words spoken by Jesus Himself. It was all for love. From the Father, Son and Holy Spirit. It was all for love. I wonder if we have even begun to fathom the depths that you and I are treasured by God?

When the stake of the cross was thrust into the earth, God staked his claimed on this planet by flying His Banner of Love for all this world to see. Jesus said, *"When the Son of Man is lifted up I will draw all men unto me"* (John 12:32).

The Gospel doesn't end at the cross. There had to be a resurrection, from death to life, from guilty to forgiven, from filthy to righteous, from slave to sons and daughters. This level of complete victory has to be experiential. God's dream was an all-consuming victory for us. Paul writes in Colossians something profound that was part of the assignment Jesus carried out in the heavenly realms on resurrection day.

"Seeing then that we have a great High Priest who has passed through the heavens, Jesus the Son of God..."
Hebrew 4:14

"...He has made alive together with Him, having forgiven you all trespasses, having wiped out the handwriting of requirements that was against us, whichwas contrary to us. And He has taken it out of the way, having nailed it to the cross. Having disarmed principalities and powers, He made a public spectacle of them, triumphing over them in it."
Colossians 2:13-15

Did you skip those scriptures just above? Don't. This is the revelation of victory and the kingdom coming to you in God's style. This is epic. Jesus had to ascend as our High Priest. On the Day of Atonement for the children of Israel, the high priest would enter the holy of holies in the tabernacle behind the veil, where the ark of the covenant rested — the mercy seat. Here, in an act of honor and sacred worship, the priest would take the blood of a spotless lamb and pour it onto the mercy seat to atone for the sins of Israel.

VICTORIOUS LION

This prophetic interaction between God and man spoke of a coming day when God would lovingly give His own Lamb to atone for the sins of all mankind and by a new and living covenant release grace and mercy because of the blood of Jesus.

Our High Priest passed through the heavens on assignment to enter into the throne room of God, unto the Father, to present His own blood as a testament sealing and invoking a new and living covenant between Father, Son and Spirit. Hallelujah.

Don't miss this. As Jesus *passed through the heavens* as our high priest, he *disarmed principalities and powers, He made a public spectacle of them, triumphing over them in it"* (see Colossians 2:15).

The overwhelming power and triumphant accomplishment of the cross is far beyond our human comprehension. In the heavenly realms, Jesus stripped and disarmed Satan and the demonic princes and powers of their rule and authority. Disarmed or dethroned means, "to remove from a throne or place of prominence: deposed." The word deposed means "to remove from office, position, or authority, especially high office."

Jesus' Question For Inquiring Minds

For just a moment, let me take you into a story in the Gospel of Matthew. The Bible says that Pharisees, Scribes and Sadducees had gathered around and they were inquiring Jesus about the resurrection. It was quite a comical conversation as they were trying to trap Jesus in useless riddles. As the conversation progressed, Jesus answered them concerning the greatest commandments of loving God with all that you are and loving people. Everything seemed to be going okay until Jesus dropped the bomb on them. Jesus inquired of them to speak about David's psalm concerning the identity of the Messiah found in Psalm 110. He asked a very straight-forward question about the Christ, "Whose Son is He?"

"While the Pharisees were gathered together, Jesus asked them, saying,"What do you think about the Christ? Whose Son is He?" They said to Him, "The Son of David." He said to them, "How then does David in the Spirit call Him 'Lord,' saying: 'The Lord said to my Lord, "Sit at My right hand, Till I make Your enemies Your footstool"'? If David then calls Him 'Lord,' how is

BOLD AS LIONS

He his Son?" And no one was able to answer Him a word, nor from that day on did anyone dare question Him anymore."
(Matthew 22:41-45)

In Psalm 110, David had an open vision where he sees the Father speaking to the Son and making a declaration over Him. This declaration speaks prophetically of identity, authority, power and declaring Him a priest, and the order of the priesthood that the Son would come from.

"The Lord said to my Lord, 'Sit at My right hand, Till I make Your enemies Your footstool.' The Lord shall send the rod of Your strength out of Zion. Rule in the midst of Your enemies! Your people shall be volunteers In the day of Your power; In the beauties of holiness, from the womb of the morning, You have the dew of Your youth. The Lord has sworn and will not relent,'"You are a priest forever according to the order of Melchizedek.'"
Psalm 110: 1-4

The Old Testament order of the priesthood came from the Levites. Who were the Levites? They were the sons and descendants of Levi. Who is Levi? We're not talking about blue jeans here. Levi is one of the twelve sons of Jacob. Remember Abraham had a promised son named Isaac. Isaac had a son named Jacob. Jacob had twelve sons that became twelve tribes. From the tribe of Levi came the priesthood that ministered unto the Lord in the Tabernacle. If you have your thinking cap on, which I know you do, you know that Jesus did not descend from the Tribe of Levi. And you also know that David couldn't have been confused about the order of the priesthood that had the privilege to minister unto the Lord in the Tabernacle.

Where did Jesus descend from? That's right. From the Tribe of Judah. No priest had ever come from the tribe of Judah. What was David seeing? He was seeing an old order being dismissed and a new order of priesthood coming forth. Not only was Jesus breaking ranks from the old order, but according to what David saw and prophesied, He was a *"...priest forever, according to the order of Melchizedek"*.

David didn't say Mel Gibson, he said Melchizedek. If Jesus is a Priest from the order of Melchizedek, then whom is he talking about?

In Hebrews chapters seven through nine, Paul unfolds the

revelation and identity of Melchizedek. His name means, "king of peace" and "king of righteousness." The Bible says he was both king and priest. He was King of Salem and priest of The Most High God. You may remember Abraham meeting him in the book of Genesis in the valley of the kings after Abraham had rescued his nephew, Lot, with the help of all his mighty trained men (see Genesis 14:14).

It's very interesting the mystery hidden for us, not from us, concerning Melchizedek.

"For this Melchizedek, king of Salem, priest of the Most High God, who met Abraham returning from the slaughter of the kings and blessed him, to whom also Abraham gave a tenth part of all, first being translated "king of righteousness," and then also king of Salem, meaning "king of peace," without father, without mother, without genealogy, having neither beginning of days nor end of life, but made like the Son of God, remains a priest continually" (Hebrews 7:1-4).

Melchizedek is shrouded in mystery as the King of Salem and Priest of The Most High God. "Jeru" means "city of" and "Salem" means "peace." Add them together. Jerusalem. Jerusalem means, "city of peace."

What does Melchizedek's name mean? "King of Peace" and "King of righteousness". This Melchizedek encounters Abraham in Genesis chapter fourteen. After Abraham's victory He comes to bring him a gift of bread and wine. What is bread and wine? It is the meal of covenant and communion.

> *"Then Melchizedek king of Salem brought out bread and wine; he was the priest of God Most High. And he blessed him and said: "Blessed be Abram of God Most High, Possessor of heaven and earth; And blessed be God Most High, Who has delivered your enemies into your hand." And he gave him a tithe of all."*
> Genesis 14:18-20

Let's stop dancing around the subject — Who is Melchizedek? I believe Melchizedek is none other than Jesus, The pre-incarnate, who appeared as King of Peace and King of Righteousness from Jerusalem to make covenant with Abraham and bless Him. From this blessing and the exchange of the covenant meal, Abraham would receive the promise that kings would come forth from him. Not only kings, but a

BOLD AS LIONS

new a living priesthood according to the order of Melchizedek.

Jesus is forever King and Priest. Who's Son is He? That was the question Jesus posed for the Pharisees, Scribes and Sadducees. Here's our answer. Jesus is the Son of God, the Son of Abraham, the Son of David — The Risen Christ. He is the victorious Lion of Judah.

Inheritance of Glory

I pray, "...that the God of our Lord Jesus Christ, the Father of glory, may give to you the spirit of wisdom and revelation in the knowledge of Him, the eyes of your understanding being enlightened; that you may know what is the hope of His calling, what are the riches of the glory of His inheritance in the saints, and what is the exceeding greatness of His power toward us who believe, according to the working of His mighty power which He worked in Christ when He raised Him from the dead and seated Him at His right hand in the heavenly places, far above all principality and power and might and dominion, and every name that is named, not only in this age but also in that which is to come.

And He put all things under His feet, and gave Him to be head over all things to the church, which is His body, the fullness of Him who fills all in all."
Ephesians 1:17-23

This High Priest *who passed through the heavens,* had a promise from His own Father, *"His enemies would be made His footstool."* He would be seated high above in supremacy at the right hand of God. Jesus passed through the heavens as our high priest, *"disarming principalities and powers, He made a public spectacle of them, triumphing over them in it."* These enemies were no match for the Lion. It's impossible for Him to have enemies, because He has no equal.

After stripping and dismantling Satan and all his demonic princes of their authority and rule, Jesus ascended into the Holy of Holies that could only be accessed by the Priest of God. In the Throne Room of His Father, He presented His own blood for a new covenant. But remember, we were there too, in Christ. When He ascended, we ascended.

*"But God, who is rich in mercy, because of His great love with which
He loved us, even when we were dead in trespasses, made us
alive together with Christ (by grace you have been saved),
and raised us up together, and made us
sit together in the heavenly places in Christ Jesus,
that in the ages to come He might
show the exceeding riches of His grace in His
kindness toward us in Christ Jesus."*
Ephesians 2:4-7

Another Commission
"Peace to you! As the Father has sent Me, I also send you."
John 20:21

Doesn't all of this change everything about our present reality? Yes, it does. This gospel of glory is the victory that overcomes the world. This gospel is the commission of sons and daughters born into the Kingdom for such a time as this.

Upon returning to Jerusalem, Jesus met Mary and His disciples just as He promised at the garden tomb that morning. He revealed Himself to them. They touched his wounds, held Him in their arms. He ate with them, laughed with them and opened their hearts and spirit to the revelation of the Risen Christ.

After forty days of appearing on the earth, it was time for Him to ascend once again unto his Father. He told them he was going away to prepare a place for them and that He would surely return one day. They were told to wait in Jerusalem for the Holy Spirit's arrival. In an upper room, one hundred and twenty gathered for ten days. Jesus told them, *"But you shall receive power when the Holy Spirit comes upon you; and you shall be witnesses unto Me in Jerusalem, and in all Judea and Samaria, and to the ends of the earth"* (Acts 1:8).

On the day of Pentecost, suddenly the Holy Spirit descended upon them in great glory and burning fire. The wind and sound of heaven blew into Jerusalem enveloping those that were lingering, waiting, watching, and anticipating for the Promise. A baptism of holy fire ignited their hearts and danced upon their heads as they all spokewith heavenly tongues (see Acts 2:2-13).

This was a day like no other day in human history. It was always

BOLD AS LIONS

the desire of the Victorious Lion to throw His Holy Fire upon the earth (see Luke 12:49). This inheritance of glory is ours. His commission will send and carry you where you have never dreamed.

I hear Him roaring. I hear Him calling out to you and to me right now. He's saying, Who will go for us? The Lion roars, Whom Shall I send?

May your heart take courage, may your soul be ignited. May your voice shake the heavens and earth to cry out, "Lord, Here I Am, Send Me!"

> *"Declare his glory among the nations, his marvelous works among all the peoples! For great is the Lord, and greatly to be praised. Ascribe to the Lord, O families of the peoples, ascribe to the Lord glory and strength! Ascribe to the Lord the glory due his name!"*
> Psalm 96:3, 7-8

Chapter 2

COURAGE
In An Age Of Compromise & Conformity

*"Expecting the world to treat you kindly because you are good
is like expecting a bull not to charge you because you're a vegetarian."*
C.S. Lewis

    This book is called, BOLD AS LIONS. This is not, "Chicken Noodle Soup For The Soul." I hope you're hungry and desperate for God. If not, you may want to take a deep breath before reading this chapter or the remainder of this book. There's a focus and burning intensity within this book, and it is specifically for those who long for an uncommon depth and more meaningful place in God.
    The Holy Spirit is after cities and nations. This means He's after our hearts to fully consume us and prioritize our lifestyle, prayer life and plans to follow His agenda. With the assignment we are called to carry, we don't have the luxury of holding onto our lives. When you follow the Lion, you deny yourself. That is what true courage is.
    We are coming to an epic crescendo of time called the "harvest" and the "end of an age." The harvest is when seeds have grown to full maturity and they are ready for reaping.
    In Matthew chapter thirteen, Jesus presents us with a parable of the kingdom. *"The kingdom of heaven is like a man who sowed good seed in his field; but while men slept, his enemy came and sowed tares among the*

wheat and went his way. But when the grain had sprouted and produced a crop, then the tares also appeared. So the servants of the owner came and said to him, 'Sir, did you not sow good seed in your field? How then does it have tares?' He said to them, 'An enemy has done this.' The servants said to him, 'Do you want us then to go and gather them up?' But he said, 'No, lest while you gather up the tares you also uproot the wheat with them. Let both grow together until the harvest, and at the time of harvest I will say to the reapers, "First gather together the tares and bind them in bundles to burn them, but gather the wheat into my barn."'"

Later in Matthew thirteen, we learn that Jesus sends the multitude away, and He and the disciples enter into a house. Here the disciples begin to inquire and ask questions concerning the parable of the sower, the field and the seeds.

"He who sows the good seed is the Son of Man. The field is the world, the good seeds are the sons of the kingdom, but the tares are the sons of the wicked one. The enemy who sowed them is the devil, the harvest is the end of the age, and the reapers are the angels. Therefore as the tares are gathered and burned in the fire, so it will be at the end of this age. The Son of Man will send out His angels, and they will gather out of His kingdom all things that offend, and those who practice lawlessness, and will cast them into the furnace of fire. There will be wailing and gnashing of teeth. Then the righteous will shine forth as the sun in the kingdom of their Father. He who has ears to hear, let him hear!"

I believe we are witnessing before our very eyes a rapid development and maturity of all seeds that have been planted. The harvest and the end of this age is approaching. The good seeds of the kingdom are maturing into purity, power, anointing, integrity, righteousness, sacrifice, justice, truth, revelation, anointing, holiness, humility, miracles, signs and wonders.

Right along side the good crop are the tares that the enemy planted, visible for all to see: lawlessness, rage, offense, horrors, strife, envy, wrath, murder, incest, hatred, blasphemy, human trafficking, homosexuality, lesbianism and transsexuality. These seeds have grown perhaps to an epic maturity like we have never seen before in our own society. The level of intensity has openly increased dramatically. Today we have witches and satanist throughout our nation openly pronouncing curses on our President.

In this hour, you'd better get prepared for a divine confrontation

COURAGE

of the kingdom of light and the kingdom of darkness. Our times demand supernatural courage and boldness. We are racing to a tipping point. Those who will stand in the truth and speak the truth had better be prepared for the backlash. Truth is highly flammable in the culture. The clash of kingdoms couldn't be more obvious.

True reformation and revival is coming. It's going to get very messy, but its necessary. People often romanticize visions of change, but the truth is, the cost of reformation is extreme. It will cost you everything — most certainly your reputation.

If you are going to speak truth in this hostile culture you will undoubtedly be mocked and persecuted. William Booth, the founder of The Salvation Army once said, "It seems that God cannot do anything on the planet earth unless a few good men are willing to go to jail." William wasn't promoting violence. He knew the hostility and extreme resistance to the Gospel in his own culture.

It's no coincidence that most of the New Testament was written from a jail cell. The Apostle Paul was a reformer. Most of the prophets were in jail. Why? Preaching the kingdom of God brings one into conflict with earthly tyranny. Make no mistake, it's going to require tremendous courage in this hour. The mark of a true servant of God is his or her willingness to suffer shame, persecution and rejection for the Master.

The high price for standing for the truth will never be marked down or go on sale.

The prophet Isaiah was put into a hollow log and sawed in half. Jeremiah endured opposition, beatings, imprisonment and was abducted and taken to Egypt. Daniel was thrown into a lion's den. Shadrach, Meshach and Abednego were thrown into the fiery furnace because they refused to bow and worship a Babylonian false god.

John the Baptist had his head cut off and served on a platter for a party display. Jesus was a man of many sorrows and well acquainted with grief. He was lifted upon a cross and crucified in the prime of his life. Eleven of the twelve disciples died a martyr's death.

Andrew and Bartholomew were crucified. James, the son of Alphaeus, was stoned to death. James, the son of Zebedee was beheaded. His brother John was boiled in oil and banished to the island of Patmos. Peter and Philip were crucified upside down. Thomas was martyred in India. Stephen being filled with the Holy Spirit looked

BOLD AS LIONS

toward heaven, where he saw our glorious God and Jesus standing at his right side. He said, *"I see heaven open and the Son of Man standing at the right side of God!"* The council members shouted, covered their ears, attacked Stephen and dragged him out of the city where he was stoned to death. The Apostle Paul was stoned, beaten, imprisoned and finally beheaded. Church history is bloody with the sacrifice of suffering and conviction.

In First Corinthians, Paul shares how the true apostles and reformers were received by the world and the church — derided and reviled as scum. *"For I think that God has displayed us, the apostles, last, as men condemned to death; for we have been made a spectacle to the world, both to angels and to men. We are fools for Christ's sake, but you are wise in Christ! We are weak, but you are strong! You are distinguished, but we are dishonored! To the present hour we both hunger and thirst, and we are poorly clothed, and beaten, and homeless. And we labor, working with our own hands. Being reviled, we bless; being persecuted, we endure; being defamed, we entreat. We have been made as the scum of the earth, the offscouring of all things until now"* (1 Corinthians 4:9-13).

I remember when Bren and I stood quietly and reverently in the Coliseum of Rome, honoring the memory of those Christians who had been condemned to death, paying the ultimate sacrifice for their faith in Jesus. Here's the point, all who share in Christ's riches will also share in His suffering" (Philippians 3:10).

The awakening that is just beginning to break forth in this hour will surely "separate the men from the boys" so to speak. Many believers in our generation are going to have to come to grips with a certain reality. Do they possess mere preferences or deep abiding convictions? Let me tell it to you straight — it will cost you everything to courageously follow Jesus. There will be great opposition, challenges, difficulty, trials and suffering in the days and years ahead. But there is no price too great. Jesus is our Reward.

> *"Blessed are those who are persecuted for righteousess' sake, for theirs is the kingdom of heaven. Blessed are you when they revile and persecute you, and say all kinds of evil against you falsely for My sake. Rejoice and be exceedingly glad, for great is your reward in heaven, for so they persecuted the prophets who were before you."*
> Matthew 5:10-12

COURAGE

"Therefore, having been justified by faith, we have peace with God through our Lord Jesus Christ, through whom also we have access by faith into this grace in which we stand, and rejoice in hope of the glory of God. And not only that, but we also glory in tribulations, knowing that tribulation produces perseverance; and perseverance, character; and character, hope. Now hope does not lead to disappointment, because the love of God has been poured out in our hearts by the Holy Spirit who was given to us."
Romans 5:1-5

Dietrich Bonhoeffer
"Who will rise up for me against the wicked? Who will take a stand for me against evildoers?"
Psalm 94:16

My life has been deeply impacted through the courageous faith of this man. I like to think that he and I would have been great friends in life. When I think of Bonhoeffer, I can't help but think of unstoppable courage — he was truly bold as a lion.

As Adolf Hitler and his demonic Third Reich swept through a continent attempting to annihilate the Jews of Europe from the face of the earth, there was small band of brothers, anti-Nazi dissidents, who committed themselves to ambush this evil at all cost. One of these men was a prophetic voice and German Pastor, Dietrich Bonhoeffer.

Bonhoeffer's life has become a riveting profile in courage, justice, conviction and radical obedience. He was a passionate lover of Jesus, pastor, musician, brilliant theologian, and spy. Rather than fleeing from Nazi Germany, he committed his life, knowing death was certain. Bonhoeffer faced a level of social, political and religious intimidation that very few ever encounter. Much has been written about his involvement with the famous "Operation Valkyrie" plot to try and assassinate Hitler and his involvement with "Operation 7," the effort to smuggle Jews into Switzerland. His response to the call of God and his unyielding passion for truth sets him apart and defines courage.

Dietrich was one of the first Germans to oppose Adolf Hitler during his rise to power, and to openly support the Jewish people. Instead of cowering down and bowing to the Nazis, he stood virtually alone in calling for the church's resistance to the persecution of Jews.

He was born February 4, 1906 in Breslau, Germany. At the age of fourteen, he shared with his family that it was in his heart and destiny to become a pastor. You can imagine they were stunned with his announcement because his family rarely went to church. He graduated with honors from the University of Berlin in 1924. In 1930, he came to America (New York City) for his postgraduate studies both studying and teaching at NYC Union Theological Seminary.

Hitler became chancellor in January 1933. Two days later, Dietrich delivered a radio address attacking Hitler and fiercely warning Germany against slipping into the idolatrous cult of the Führer (leader) who could very well turn out to be Verführer (mis-leader or seducer). His speech was cut short from the radio in mid-sentence.

By September that year, the German Evangelical Church adopted racist Nazi policies, which led to Dietrich receiving a ministry assignment in London. Dietrich stood opposed to the German Christian movement that was incorporating Nazi racism into the Christian gospel. The struggle within the church was clear; the "National Church" supported Hitler and the "Confessing Church" believed that Hitler could in no way be their leader. The heresy, deception and apostasy of the National Church was straight out of the pit of hell. Read these words carefully: *"The time is fulfilled for the German people of Hitler. It is because of Hitler that Christ, God the helper and redeemer, has become effective among us. ... Hitler is the way of the Spirit and the will of God for the German people to enter the Church of Christ."* These are the words of German pastor Hermann Gruner. Another German pastor put it more succinctly: *"Christ has come to us through Adolph Hitler."*

Bonhoeffer, along with Martin Niemoller and Karl Barth did all they could to rally support in the Confessing Church movement against the Nazis. These lion-hearts drafted the famous "Barmen Confession of Faith" in which they associated 'Hitlerism' with idolatry. As you can imagine, it made them a sure target for the Gestapo. As the demons of war and mind manipulation crept forward to annihilate the purity of the church, a bishop, Theodor Heckel, in charge of foreign affairs, traveled to London and sharply warned Dietrich to abstain from any activity that wasn't directly authorized by Berlin. The lion-heart refused the intimidation. He chose to stand almost alone as the Confessing Church aided the Jews.

COURAGE

The intensity of Nazi suppression grew stronger against the Confessing Church and also led to Dietrich's authorization to teach being revoked in 1936. Even as the intimidation and threats of the Gestapo grew worse, it did not stop him from taking necessary risks to voice his convictions. He would often quote Proverbs 31:8, *"Who will speak up for those who are voiceless?"* It was his burning passion that had to voice defending the Jews in Nazi Germany.

As Bonhoeffer was teaching in the seminary at Finkenwalde, he wrote his brilliant and now famous books, "The Cost of Discipleship," and "Life Together." The Gestapo shut down this seminary in October 1937. Bonhoeffer kept moving forward trying to conduct a secret "seminary on the run," always moving from village to village, meeting and training Confessing Church pastors. They literally risked their lives to pray together, study together, and live together. Over time, this too was unsuccessful. The sustained pressure from the Gestapo caused the Confessing Church pastors to begin to waver and many of them sought out legitimacy from the government in return for peace and security.

Throughout a series of strategic events, Deitrick became an agent of the Military Intelligence Department and provided information to Allied agents that were working in hopes to assassinate Hitler. What was not widely known was that it was also the center of the anti-Hitler resistance. He was functioning as a double agent. His mission was to scout intelligence information through his "pastoral visits" and ecumenical connections. Under cover, Bonhoeffer was involved in secret courier activities. His principal mission was to seek terms of surrender from the Allies, should an "Abwehr proposed plot" against Hitler succeed.

Dietrich was finally arrested on April 5, 1943, and imprisoned as a spy suffering for nearly two years being tortured and brutally interrogated. He was sent to Tegel prison, then the concentration camps of Buchenwald and Flossenburg. During his imprisonment, Dietrich befriended prison guards, who brought him books filled with coded communications from his family and fiancé. He also began writing "Ethics," an expression of his courageous beliefs. Through his life and courageous faith, even the prison guards hearts became so tender that one even offered to help him escape, but Dietrich chose not to run, knowing his imprisoned family members would suffer the Nazi's wrath.

By April 1945, Hitler had survived fifteen assisination attempts on his life, Berlin was in total ruin, and the Germans knew they had lost the war. As the orders came to kill the resistance, one of Hitler's special commandos in Flossenburg stripped Dietrich and hanged him in the nude. The lion-heart pastor was only 39 years young.

History tells us that three weeks later, Patton's army came victoriously and Hitler committed suicide as the American forces liberated Flossenburg. On May 7th, the war in Europe was over.

What can we learn from Bonhoeffer? What is his legacy? I could spend the rest of this book trying to unfold those truths. His discernment was key from the beginning. He had the courage to immediately speak out against the threat that he saw rising in National Socialism. That took incredible bravery — ultimately costing his life. Many other German Pastors were either seduced by the Nazis or were bullied and cowered into silence.

After the war was over, Martin Niemoller, famously said: *"In Germany the Nazi's came first for the communists and I didn't speak up because I wasn't a communist. Then they came for the Jews and I didn't speak up because I wasn't a Jew. Then they came for the Trade Unionists and I didn't speak up because I wasn't a Trade Unionist. Then they came for the Catholics and I didn't speak up because I was a Protestant. Then they came for me and by that time there was no one left to speak up."*

What we learn from Bonhoeffer is that he spoke up at the very start. He was willing to be a prophetic voice to his nation, running counter culture and placing himself out of step with the rise of German nationalism. There were Pastors at the time who claimed the church should submit to the authorities and be guided by them in how they functioned, appealing to Scriptures: *"Let every soul be subject unto the higher powers. For there is no power but of God: the powers that be are ordained of God. Whosoever therefore resists the power, resists the ordinance of God: and they that resist shall receive to themselves damnation"* (Romans 13:1-2).

For Bonhoeffer, taking this position was completely unacceptable and twisting the Scriptures. He believed that submission was never to mean an uncritical, unconditional, blind obedience and acceptance. In fact, in certain conditions it will not include obedience at all, but rather a conscientious disobedience.

COURAGE

Bonhoeffer said, "I love my country and will give to it everything excepting one thing; my conscience. That belongs to the Kingdom of God and when they clash my conscience will bow only to the Kingdom of God." He knew that "rendering unto Caesar the things that are Caesar's" doesn't mean giving to Caesar all the things he asks for. The arbiter of what belongs to Caesar is not Caesar but God. Dietrick Bonhoeffer reminds us all that the true Church of Christ will always, to one degree or another, be out of step with the society it is placed in. Like Jesus, we too will be culturally offensive to the ruling elites.

Bonhoeffer was prepared as a young man to pay the price that most prophetic voices end up paying for moral and ethical clarity. Where are our bold lions today? Where is the unstoppable spirit who knows there is no price too great for Christ? Where are the consecrated and courageous leaders that confront the corruption, heresy and apostasy creeping into the church in this hour? Sadly, ministries in our Nation can hardly stand in the pulpit and speak with confidence and courage the word of God concerning homosexuality, abortion, racism, pornography, ect. They've bought into the lie of political correctness. They're bound by the fear of man and their obsession to build or maintain their crowds and followers. There must be a new breed of young lions — young leaders who refuse to play it safe — who will love God with all their heart, soul, mind and strength (Matthew 22:37). They will not be stopped, even if they are persecuted, mocked, arrested, placed in jail, or martyred. They will be unashamedly bold and holy!

Perhaps one of the most valuable lessons of Bonhoeffer's life that Christian men and women in our times desperately need is a lesson in obedience—a virtue that's highly unpopular and largely absent from our present culture. Bonhoeffer was a lion-heart. He was serious about his faith in Christ. He could not afford to be.

(Lastly, if you have never heard of Bonhoeffer until picking up Bold As Lions, I want to encourage you to pick up his epic book, "The Cost of Discipleship" also, "Life Together", "Letters & Papers from Prison" and "Ethics". I also highly recommend, "Bonhoeffer: Pastor, Martyr, Prophet, Spy" released in 2010 by Eric Metaxes).

BOLD AS LIONS

William Tyndale
1494 – 1536
"But the righteous are bold as a lion."
Proverbs 28:1

What does raw courage and an unquenchable heart look like? Look at the legacy and burning passions of the lion-heart named, William Tyndale. William was a passionate Christian, a watchman, a gifted scholar, an ordained priest, and he was educated at Oxford University. He saw firsthand the universal corruption within the Roman Catholic Church.

In his day, Rome held the ultimate power, presiding its rule even over kings and governments. The Pope and his bishops believed they were incapable of err in all spiritual matters. The core belief was and still is, that the Church Tradition holds equal, if not more authority than the Holy Bible. For William, the infallible, inerrant word of God, The Holy Bible, was this reformer's final authority. Just as Peter and other Apostles were hunted down, William knew his allegiance was to God rather than men.

The spiritual climate of his nation was sterile and barren. The Roman Catholic Church went to extreme measures to prevent the ordinary common people from having any independent understanding of the Bible — particularly in what is said concerning their beliefs of purgatory, transubstantiation, confession of sins to priests, selling of indulgences, praying to Mary, praying to saints, salvation by works, and the never ending demand for money.

In direct defiance to the Pope's law, William laid a foundation of the New Testament from the original Greek. This translation was far different from the Roman Catholic Church's official Latin Vulgate version. His resistance to the Pope marked him as going rogue and unleashed the full wrath and rage of the Papacy. He was hunted down much like David fleeing from the demonized fury of King Saul.

William knew it was illegal to translate the Bible into English, the language of the common person. In those days, only the clergy were allowed to have the scriptures. But after seeing people wander aimlessly without truth, after talking with priests who knew very little of the Bible themselves, William went about making copies of his version in English and getting the Word out to as many people as possible.

COURAGE

This was his passion and divine assignment. His dream and mission, if successful, was that the boy plowing the fields, who owned a Bible would know more than the priests of the time.

Back in the fourteenth century, John Wycliffe was the first to make (or at least oversee) an English translation of the Bible, but that was before the invention of the printing press and all copies had to be hand written. The church had banned the unauthorized translation of the Bible into English in 1408 that strictly "forbade anyone to translate, or even read, any parts of vernacular versions of the Bible, without express episcopal permission," which Tyndale courageously refused. As he was being persecuted by England Catholic Bishops, he fled for his life as the King's agents chased him all over Europe, and he printed thousands of copies. Six thousand copies were printed and smuggled into England.

In May of 1535, William was captured and incarcerated for sixteen months. He was imprisoned at Vilvoorde Castle located in Belgium. Here he was examined, interrogated, threatened and demanded to recant. He would not. Most of us cannot even begin to contemplate the suffering this man endured. On October 6, 1536, at age 42, William Tyndale was chained to the stake, strangled and then burned alive to ashes. His last breaths were used to pray for the King of England's eyes to be opened. Amazingly, his prayer was answered in 1539, when Henry VIII decreed that an English Bible should be made available in the churches of England. We are still reading William's work today as 90 percent of the New Testament in the King James Version is his. Without question, Tyndale's first printed New Testament became the basis of all future English translations.

William was no criminal. He was a faithful pioneer, a reformer, a messenger of hope and deliverance, who dreamed of his generation and generations yet to come to encounter Jesus in the life-giving Word of God. His greatest criminal charge was that he believed *"in the forgiveness of sins and that the mercy offered in the gospel was enough for salvation."* Can you imagine that being your death charge?

Today, more than four centuries later, we owe a debt of gratitude and honor to the man that gave his own life so that we could access the transforming word of God. Through the scriptures we have been given the blue prints for culture in shaping history and society — stories, poetry, praise and prophecies, the history of mankind, and the revelation of God's great love, of Jesus Christ and the indwelling Holy Spirit - grace, salvation and empowerment for His children.

Francis Asbury
The Revivalist, Abolitionist
& Prophet Of The Long Road

Recently, I was in Washington, D.C. once again for a special ministry assignment. I made my way just a few blocks north of the White House to sit in the park at the Francis Asbury Memorial. It was a special time for me to reflect on the life of this lion-heart and revivalist who invested his calling and his soul into the spiritual foundation and DNA of the United States of America. Asbury sits high on his tired and battered horse. He's dressed as a frontiersmen, in his riding boots, hat and cape holding his Bible and messages in his hand. The inscription on the Statue reads:

"IF YOU SEEK THE RESULTS OF HIS LABOR YOU WILL FIND THEM IN OUR CHRISTIAN CIVILIZATION"

"HIS CONTINUOUS JOURNEYS THROUGH CITIES, VILLAGES AND SETTLEMENTS FROM 1771 TO 1816 GREATLY PROMOTED PATRIOTISM, EDUCATION, MORALITY AND RELIGION IN THE AMERICAN REPUBLIC."

"FRANCIS ASBURY 1745-1816
PIONEER METHODIST BISHOP IN AMERICA"

On the back of the statue you find these words:
"THE PROPHET OF THE LONG ROAD"

In studying revival history, you will find that Francis is considered the father of the American "circuit riders" who helped shape our Christian culture. The circuit riders were the powerhouse itinerant preachers on horseback that carried the Gospel of Jesus Christ throughout the wilderness terrain of America's colonies.

Through the ministry and leadership of John Wesley, Methodism was a burning torch during England's dark and immoral

COURAGE

age. The Wesleys spread spiritual renewal and revival throughout England, Scotland and Ireland. John and Charles Wesley, along with their friend George Whitefield became catalysts in spreading the Great Awakening to America. The Wesley brothers had a profound impact upon young Asbury. In August 1771, John Wesley rose in their Annual Conference in the City of Bristol looking for young lions to commission as he shouted, *"Our brethren in America call aloud for help. Who will go?"* A young British preacher only 26-year-old courageously stood to answer the call of a missionary. Francis Asbury's decision that day would launch him into a lifelong call that would dramatically impact the spiritual destiny of America.

The call of God required Francis to leave his family, his childhood friends, his girlfriend and his fellow workers in the intense iron-working region in the midlands of England. His assignment was to cross the Atlantic Ocean and to preach the Gospel to the thirteen American colonies. In time, his itinerant preaching became a regiment that included more than six-thousand miles on horseback every year. In his forty-five-year ministry to America he covered more than a quarter million miles on horseback through the wilderness. It's hard to fathom this kind of passion and intensity – and would be literally impossible without the holy burnings of God freshly ablaze in your heart.

The life on the evangelistic trail for Asbury was not filled with plush hotels, hot showers, Uber services, generous preaching honorariums or great meals and hospitality. This revivalist faced the open frontier with the dangers of wolves, extreme weather, eaten up by chiggers and ticks, surviving often on bread and water alone. This circuit rider shared the company of his horse and trusted the Holy Spirit to keep him alive to preach the Gospel.

Inside the saddlebags of Asbury and the circuit riders, you would not only find their Bibles, their hand-written sermons and hymnals, but you would also find the petitions and legal forms for the freeing of slaves. For the circuit riders, being a revivalist and abolitionist was one in the same. It was no contradiction for them to approach both church and state issues openly with the life giving power of the Gospel. They burned with a desire for emancipation for the oppressed. They were not afraid to engage the cultural fight for true liberty and biblical justice.

Across the United States, you will find towns, cities, hospitals, homes and schools from Maine to south Georgia and beyond with the name Francis Asbury attached to their identity. This pioneer carried the burning message that God's love can be experienced by everyone; and that once it becomes experiential, the Holy Spirit takes up residence in your life.

Not only was Asbury a forerunner of the Gospel and revival, he carried the mantle and passion of a true abolitionist. One of the haunting questions our founding fathers wrestled over was the issue of slavery.

God raised Francis up as a prophet of truth and righteousness to condemn the injustice and oppression of slavery. Few realize the pivotal role that he played. Francis once met with President George Washington, urging him to sign an emancipation for slaves. His leadership on the slavery issue was instrumental in forming and advancing the abolitionist movement in the nation. Think about this, God, who is not limited by time or space, could see a brutal and bloody Civil War coming in America's near future that would claim the lives of more than 600,000 people, and nearly destroying our new nation. The abolitionist prophets like Francis Asbury were God's mercy strategy, providing an opportunity to avert bloodshed and disaster.

Time and time again, the Holy Spirit has highlighted to me and some of my closest ministry friends, the unmistakable similarities between how the American church and the nation as a whole have dealt with the issue of slavery and how we are presently dealing with the issue of abortion.

Our culture has dehumanized the unborn. The death culture of abortion has become a money-making industry disposing of more than 55+ million human souls and destinies. We have ignored the silent screams, torture and pain of our own children. They've been denied a voice. America had to come to understand that slavery and acts of racism is such a deplorable crime against humanity. How we ever got to the decision that allows women to take the lives of their own children through abortion is still baffling to me.

Just as slavery had to be condemned and banished, there must be a moral outcry against inhumane and repulsive murder of innocent children. Let me go on the record here. My prayer is that in our lifetime we will see abortion abolished and the curse of innocent bloodshed removed from our nation. I further believe that this tipping point will

COURAGE

become a catalyst for national reformation.

The measure of impact that Francis Asbury's life as a revivalist and abolitionist will never be fully realized until the light of eternity. We owe a great debt to this pioneer. His legacy has deeply impacted me and calls out to this generation afresh. I believe with all my heart, we are entering a true Third Great Awakening. I believe that God desires to raise up modern-day revivalists and abolitionists who will burn with the same fervor and convictions as Asbury.

"Christianity was never designed by God to make a lot of weaklings. It was designed to bring forth a race of men who were bold and strong and pure and good...Christianity is a strong mans gospel."
John G. Lake 1870 -1935

It takes profound courage to die for your faith and perhaps sometimes, more courage to live for it. Our country needs men and women of courage. Ladies, Christianity is a strong woman's gospel too. It's time for our bold lions and lionesses to arise in holy fire and supernatural courage. The nations need those who possess a courage that is born of The Spirit and are willing to become pioneers of a new day.

Follow the Holy Spirit wherever he leads you. Be Bold. Be Strong. The Lord is with you – He is in you. With the assignment we are called to carry, we don't have the luxury of holding onto our lives. When you follow the Lion, you deny yourself. That is what true courage is.

BOLD AS LIONS

Chapter 3

INTEGRITY & HONOR
The Call of the Noble

"You shall love the Lord your God with all your heart, with all your soul, and with all your mind. This is the first and great commandment. And the second is like it: You shall love your neighbor as yourself. On these two commandments hang all the Law and the Prophets."
Matthew 22:37-39

What if your consecration and commitment to integrity and honor unto the Lord could shape the course of history? This is where it all begins – this our anchor, foundation, the cornerstone, the pillars to which all integrity and honor stands secure. Loving God with everything you are — *with all your heart, with all your soul, and with all your mind.* To belong to God is to belong to His heart. The way of integrity is the way of love, intimacy, honor, passion and sacrifice.

The purity of our love and devotion unto The Father, Jesus and The Holy Spirit will determine the depth of our integrity and honor.

Integrity is the quality of being honest and having strong moral principles; moral uprightness. Integrity is possessing moral character, principle, virtue, decency, fairness, truthfulness and trustworthiness. Integrity is also defined as the state of being whole and undivided.

Honor is quality of high respect or esteem. It is a distinction of nobility, recognition, quality or effect. Honor is a life that fulfills, observes, keeps, obeys, heeds and follows. A man or a woman of honor embodies integrity and character.

> King David prayed, *"Create in me a clean heart, O God, And renew a steadfast spirit within me. Do not cast me away from Your presence, And do not take Your Holy Spirit from me."* *" Have mercy upon me, O God, according to Your lovingkindness; According to the multitude of Your tender mercies, Blot out my transgressions. Wash me thoroughly from my iniquity, And cleanse me from my sin."*
> Psalm 51:10, 1&2

Integrity and honor are two of the most vital keys that the church must recapture in this hour. In the last three decades, the Church has been riddled with scandal. We need radical healing and reformation. It is time that we all drill down deep into the core of our spirit and soul and weigh out the matter and the measures of these two sacred virtues. The world is in desperate need of the church to rediscover its glory, purity and nobility.

In today's church culture there is no shortage of conferences. There are conferences on practically everything you can imagine — the prophetic, the apostolic, the five-fold ministry, worship, the supernatural, evangelism, activating the gifts, church growth, ect. You get the point. My hope is that in this hour we would experience a strategic shift and focus on the weighty matter of personal integrity, purity, holiness and honor. Let's be honest, without this, we have nothing.

The Apostle Peter wrote, *"For the time is come that judgment must begin at the house of God: and if it first begin with us, what shall the end be of them that obey not the gospel of God?"* (1 Peter 4:17).

It is no secret that sexual immorality and financial impropriety have wounded, hurt and offended so many lives in the Body of Christ. It is sobering and painfully obvious that for the most part the mockery from the world is warranted.

There is such great need for leaders and all believers to build lives of integrity, and to build an atmosphere and culture of honor that is genuine, transparent and truthful. The Holy Spirit cannot be fooled. He is the Spirit of Truth. His character and nature is to cleanse and purify. That is the Holy Spirit's ministry.

INTEGRITY & HONOR

God Will Cleanse With Fire

"Repent, for the kingdom of heaven is at hand!" For this is he who was spoken of by the prophet Isaiah, saying: "The voice of one crying in the wilderness: 'Prepare the way of the Lord; Make His paths straight.'"

"And even now the ax is laid to the root of the trees. Therefore every tree which does not bear good fruit is cut down and thrown into the fire. I indeed baptize you with water unto repentance, but He who is coming after me is mightier than I, whose sandals I am not worthy to carry. He will baptize you with the Holy Spirit and fire. His winnowing fan is in His hand, and He will thoroughly clean out His threshing floor, and gather His wheat into the barn; but He will burn up the chaff with unquenchable fire."
Matthew 3:2&3 & 10-12

Whoa, the ax is laid at the roots. The Holy Spirit's ministry has intensity to it. You may or may not have been told the whole truth concerning the Holy Spirit. Many Christians can only relate to Jesus as the Lamb — gentle, loving, sensitive, meek and tender. But when it comes to encountering the power and fire of the Lion, they're not so sure about that. The Lion is fierce. His Spirit is fierce - meaning: aggressive, intense, burning, forceful, violent and powerful. Perhaps we need a new and fresh introduction to The Holy Spirit.

Sometimes Loving God Means Hating Evil
"The fear of the Lord is to hate evil..."
Proverbs 8:13

I realize that no matter what I say here, I'm going to offend someone. That's not my objective. However, I have laid aside the fantasy that everyone is going to like me or applaud the message. I'm well acquainted with the sufferings that messengers must endure.

The fear of Lord is to hate evil. It's a strong word, and yet, it is a word we must embrace and receive. There can be no more passivity. I believe that until we hate sickness and disease robbing from lives, we will never cry out in prayer for God to use us in healing and miracles. Until we begin to hate poverty and lack stealing from lives, we will never cry out for God to use us to bring people into abundance and prosperity. Frankly, until we begin to hate the sin in our own lives, we will just go on tolerating it. Passivity must be given no place.

You may think, "Brian, that's really strong." Sickness and disease are evil. Poverty and lack are evil. Sin is evil. We can't go on tolerating what Jesus came to liberate us from. He came that we would have abundant life.

It has been said that, "What one generation tolerates, another will celebrate." Joseph Caryl, said, "According to the weight of the burden that grieves you, is the cry to God that comes from you." I wonder; are we grieved? Have we insulated our hearts and lives so much that we cannot stop and pause our lives and contemplate what the lack of integrity and honor has done to rob each generation and the consequence that has robbed God from pouring out the blessings He longed to give.

Be Holy
God says, "Be holy, for I am holy."
1 Peter 1:16

What if your consecration and commitment to integrity and honor unto the Lord could shape the course of history? It can and it will. Our integrity can empower the future. God is calling us as men and women, fathers and mothers to integrity. We cannot afford to be lazy in our high calling of God. We must teach our natural and spiritual children how to partner with the Holy Spirit and yield to His voice. We must train and equip them to be discerning, prayerful, powerful and supernatural. The years ahead of us demand a reformation generation. In all these matters, at the top of our list in loving God with all of our hearts, soul, mind and strength, must be a call to integrity, purity and honor.

Our children are a living message that we will send to a time and place we will never see. Those that God is preparing in this hour truly need the courageous and prophetic voices of spiritual fathers and mothers. Huldah, was a prophetess that gave prophetic hope and encouragement to young King Josiah as God prepared him to destroy the idols of his day. Her heart of mercy and compassion propelled Josiah to cleans the temple. (see 2 Kings 22; 2 Chronicles 34)

INTEGRITY & HONOR

Mothers and fathers in the Lord; be courageous. This young generation needs you more than ever. Set the example, raise the standard, live with integrity and give this gift as your legacy.

Come Out From The World

You never influence and impact the world by trying to be like it. Decisions become easier when your will to please God outweighs your will to please the world. In 2 Corinthians chapter six, the Apostle Paul speaks openly concerning the call for our lives to be set apart and holy unto the Lord. This is a call to honor and to come out from the world.

"You are not restricted by us, but you are restricted by your own affections. Now in return for the same (I speak as to children), you also be open. Do not be unequally yoked together with unbelievers. For what fellowship has righteousness with lawlessness? And what communion has light with darkness? And what accord has Christ with Satan? Or what part has a believer with an unbeliever?

And what agreement has the temple of God with idols? For you are the temple of the living God. As God has said: "I will dwell in them And walk among them. I will be their God, And they shall be My people."

Therefore "Come out from among them And be separate, says the Lord. Do not touch what is unclean, And I will receive you." "I will be a Father to you, And you shall be My sons and daughters, Says the Lord Almighty." Therefore, having these promises, beloved, let us cleanse ourselves from all filthiness of the flesh and spirit, perfecting holiness in the fear of God."
2 Corinthians 6:12-7:1

The call of our Father is to come out and be set apart from the world, and have no agreement with the spirit of this world. In all these questions we see the obvious answer — there is no agreement or union with the Spirit of God and the spirit of the world. We are called to be sons and daughters that honor the Lord and aim our lives at holiness.

Purity, integrity and holiness are not "old fashioned." Integrity and example matters greatly. The world is changed by your example. Your character is your life's unending message of hope to the world.

When Paul wrote Timothy, he reminded him, *"Let no one despise your youth, but be an example to the believers in word, in conduct, in love, in spirit, in faith, in purity"* (1 Timothy 4:12).

Our character and integrity reveal the blooming person within. To grow and steward integrity, it is vital that you secure your personal vows and convictions unto The Lord and give no place for compromise.

Accountability starts with you. Leadership begins with leading yourself. You must practice and activate truth with yourself first. It is lofty and immature not to recognize that there is no exemption from sexual temptation. One of the keys to maintaining consistent victory is to fearlessly give oneself to men or women of uncommon character, who will guard and foster transparency and humility.

While many are working hard to manage their image, God is calling us to manage our integrity and character. It is time for you to place the highest value on building your community of covenant keeping friends. Perhaps God will use you to pioneer a team of winners that burn zealously for holiness. Together, we can prevail triumphantly.

Remember this, those who despise accountability and covenant faithfulness will reap the results of that in their lives. Those who love honor, loyalty and covenant faithfulness will be richly rewarded.

The Narrow Road & The Broad Road
(Taken from my first book: "Unstoppable & Unquenchable Fire")

After Jesus' unprecedented message from the "Sermon on the Mount" in Matthew Chapters 5&6, He discusses two different responses to those who profess to be loyal to Him and His Word. We see this distinction from which He calls — the narrow way and the broad way.

Jesus said, *"Enter by the narrow gate; for wide is the gate and broad is the way that leads to destruction, and there are many who go in by it. Because narrow is the gate and difficult is the way which leads to life, and there are few who find it. Beware of false prophets, who come to you in sheep's clothing, but inwardly they are ravenous wolves. You will know them by their fruits. Do men gather grapes from thornbushes or figs from thistles? Even so, every good tree bears good fruit, but a bad tree bears bad fruit. A good tree cannot bear bad fruit, nor can a bad tree bear good fruit. Every tree that does not bear good fruit*

INTEGRITY & HONOR

is cut down and thrown into the fire. Therefore by their fruits you will know them."

"Not everyone who says to Me, 'Lord, Lord,' shall enter the kingdom of heaven, but he who does the will of My Father in heaven. Many will say to Me in that day, 'Lord, Lord, have we not prophesied in Your name, cast out demons in Your name, and done many wonders in Your name?' And then I will declare to them, 'I never knew you; depart from Me, you who practice lawlessness!' "Therefore whoever hears these sayings of Mine, and does them, I will liken him to a wise man who built his house on the rock: and the rain descended, the floods came, and the winds blew and beat on that house; and it did not fall, for it was founded on the rock. But everyone who hears these sayings of Mine, and does not do them, will be like a foolish man who built his house on the sand: and the rain descended, the floods came, and the winds blew and beat on that house; and it fell. And great was its fall" (Matthew 7:13-27).

The distinction Jesus makes here is painfully clear. One had a true relationship with God, the other was deceived into believing he had a relationship with God, but didn't. Jesus tragically replies, *"I never knew you."* Real freedom and liberty is not liberty apart from Jesus' leadership and authority. Freedom in the kingdom of God is not a free-for-all. There is divine order and government in the kingdom of God. True liberty is liberation from sin, defilement and things that darken our hearts. There are a lot of people in the body of Christ who claim grace, yet desire "liberties" from Jesus' commands and restraints. They want His forgiveness, but they refuse to obey the call to responsibility and holiness. That's not a biblical Christianity. Jesus is making clear that there is a false road and true road — the broad way that leads to destruction or the narrow way that leads to life. He is not contrasting the Church and the world here in this message. He is speaking to those who profess loyalty, faithfulness and authenticity in their faith, but their self-deception has them headed for eternal destruction. It's remarkable the number of people who have grown up in church and have been effectively Christianized, professing to know God, but have never genuinely met Christ. It is terrifying to think that many souls could hear these words, *"Depart from Me, I never knew you."*

The narrow way must be the highest priority of your life — to know and love the heart of God. It is about true friendship and intimacy with the Lord. God knows those who have made Him the sole passion of their hearts, and those who just profess His name, but inwardly are not joined in relationship. The heart that walks the narrow way is fearfully aware of sin's defilement and it guards itself, so that it might be presented unto the Lord as a clean and honorable vessel. Such hearts are those which *"fear The Lord and depart from evil"* (Proverbs 3:7). The narrow road is the only road in New Testament Christianity. The travelers along the narrow way look for the grace that delivers them from sin and empowers them. *"For the grace of God that brings salvation has appeared to all men, teaching us that, denying ungodliness and worldly lusts, we should live soberly, righteously, and godly in the present age..."* (Titus 2:12). Those who travel the narrow road are those who *work out their salvation with fear and trembling; for it is God who works in you both to will and to do for His good pleasure* (Philippians 2:12,13). The narrow and loyal followers of The Master are those with sincerity, who consecrate their hearts and yield their lives unto The Lord's work within them, so that they may be holy and sanctified. Holiness is not old fashion, friend. The narrow way follower is not bound by restriction, but bound by love.

The broad road is a road of tolerance, compromise and has very few restrictions. It is a road of permissiveness in the grace of God. It's wide open for many opinions, ideologies and lifestyles. On the broad road, you can keep your carry-on luggage of immorality, a little drunkenness, some slander and gossip with a hint of defamation...a little porn and lust here and there with little regard for the warnings of The Holy Spirit or repentance. The travelers along the broad road are always looking for a *grace* that covers their indulgences and pleasures, because they believe God is aware of weakness, yet his grace pardons them. The preachers of the broad road use the Bible all the time for their indulgences, yet they bear no fruits of true repentance in denying the flesh and keeping to spiritual disciplines. Moses brought us the law; but Jesus came to bring grace and truth. (see John 1:17) There's the beautiful truth and the ugly truth — remember, it's a two-edged sword. Make no mistake, grace is beautiful, but if you abuse its beauty with lawlessness, you're in danger of hell fire. Without truth, there is a distorted message, promoting a certain confidence, which allows people to continue in compromise. Jesus said their destruction will be more terrifying than they can ever imagine when they stand face to face with Him. This must not be your story.

Today we have modern grace teachers who tell us that we don't need to repent of sins, as we are under His grace. Do not be deceived, friend. Grace comes as a beautiful and marvelous gift from the heart of our Father, to those who repent of their sins and long to live in pure union with God's heart (1 John 1:9). Grace will transform you. Grace is not an invitation to fall into sin. It's an invitation to fall in Love.

If you are going to live the true grace lifestyle, the abundant life that Christ gives, you must be sure that you deny fleshly lust. To be a disciple and authentic follower of Jesus, this is paramount. Jesus said, *"Strive to enter through the narrow gate, for many, I say to you, will seek to enter and will not be able."* Strive means to make every effort of commitment. Let me be clear, we do not strive to earn God's love or forgiveness. We don't pray and fast to motivate God to love us — of course not! Christianity is not a behavioral modification, self-improvement or sin management program. It's the indwelling of the Spirit of God that transforms a life from the inside out. His ministry is unparalleled. Grace is about covenant relationship. We strive to give meaningful effort to the relationship, just as a husband does in his marriage to his wife.

As a husband, I aim and strive to strengthen the commitment and devotion my wife and I have to one another, and our children. When someone makes no effort to invest in a relationship, love could be brought into question. Our *striving* is an expression of honor and devotion, making every effort to position our hearts in alignment with Him. Then His grace can empower us over sin. We must strive with zealous determination to deny sin at all times and *give no place for the devil* (Ephesians 4:27).

It is by no means a contradiction to strive courageously to enter the narrow gate, which Jesus said comes with difficulty and challenge, and to wear His yoke, which is easy and light. Jesus was warning His hearers of the yoke of the Pharisees, which was a burdensome and oppressive yoke of self-righteousness and legalistic law keeping. Many bible scholars have said that the Pharisees had added over 600 regulations, regarding what qualified as working on the Sabbath. That is a heavy burden! The Lord's yoke is light and easy to carry, because it is the yoke of repentance and faith, followed by a singular commitment to honor Him.

Frankly, the narrow road is hard on our flesh — to overcome and deny sin — as we take up our cross and die daily. The yoke of

Jesus speaks of taking on lowliness of heart (true meekness). Jesus is inviting us into a lifestyle of dying to the things we must die to, so that we might experience His yoke of liberation.

This is the narrow way. It's not a popular message, but it's the only biblical message of true grace. Grace leads to real life and a vibrant heart. For those who *fear the Lord and depart from evil,* the promise remains true: *...it will be health to your flesh and strength to your bones* (Proverbs 3:7&8). Striving to fully honor Jesus will lead to the abundant life, eternal reward and true encounters with The Lord. This is the fruit of true love.

"Not that I have already obtained all this, or have already arrived at my goal; But I am pressing on, striving to take hold of that for which Christ Jesus took hold of me."
Philippians 3:12

As sons and daughters of God, it should be our daily aim and our lifelong pursuit to strive to honor the grace of our Father. Paul urged the church to *"aim for perfection"* (2 Corinthians 13:11). Dear friend, in our pursuit, let us remember these urgent and passionate words from Paul: *"We then, as workers together with Him also plead with you not to receive the grace of God in vain"* (2 Corinthians 6:1).

Honor, Humility & Holiness

A lifestyle of honor will be the pathway for opening doors for you and for others that you love — doors and opportunities that may have never been possible without honor. Honor will also open doors that look ridiculous to the natural eye, but remember, sometimes the door to the miraculous looks ridiculous on the outside. Don't be afraid to walk through the doors that honor creates.

Honor attracts the anointing. Humility sustains the anointing. Holiness protects the anointing. Cherish the anointing of The Holy Spirit in your life, and the Holy Spirit will honor and favor you in life. Our consciousness of His abiding presence within determines our level of consecration and integrity.

The Holy Spirit desires to identify to you the great value and purpose of others. It is worth taking risks for the sake of another's prophetic destiny. Abigail recognized God's calling upon King David and risked her life to see it come to pass. Her selflessness and honor opened the door for influence, and so can yours. Be aware of the prophetic destinies of those around you. Be courageous in order to pull out the greatness of others. Recognize that you have the power to bring solutions to the most difficult problems. Honor, humility and holiness are the real source to kingdom solutions. I like to say, "God is in the details" (see 1 Samuel 25:13-33).

A Lifestyle of Prayer & Fasting
The Key to Integrity

God never intended for us to be weak, timid or cowering. He desired for us to reveal His fierce love. That's why He placed the gift of His Spirit within us, so that we would become sons and daughters that are bold as lions. Keeping your integrity will make you bold and sharp. Your integrity will make you effective and give you longevity and quality of life and ministry.

Operating in the grace of God is not a fragile man's sport. It requires strength and intensity. Honoring the grace of God and keeping our integrity will cause us to stand in an hour when many are bowing low to the spirit of this age. God is calling you and I to stand. It's time to pray for courage, develop integrity and live responsibly.

The Holy Spirit never calls anyone into a "season" of fasting and prayer. He doesn't call anyone into a "season" of revival. However, the Holy Spirit does invite and calls us all into a "lifestyle" of fasting, prayer and unending revival. What we gain by fasting and prayer, we keep through fasting and prayer.

Fasting will keep you sharp and sharpen your integrity. A soldier is sharp. A soldier stays fit, alert, healthy and ready. They're not dull, casual nor complacent. A soldier is not asleep on their watch. The Apostle Paul said that we should live in such a way as a soldier because the days are evil. The enemy is hungry and lurking for an opportune moment of attack. Colossians 4:2 says, *"Continue steadfastly in prayer, being watchful in it with thanksgiving."*

A soldier is a watchman. Throughout all of Scripture you can see time and time again the method of fasting sharpens a life. Moses fasted. Elijah fasted forty days. Paul fasted fourteen days. Jesus fasted forty days.

God wants us spiritually sharp and physically ready, fit and alert. Fasting will sharpen your spiritual perception and discernment. A lifestyle of fasting can keep you spiritually alert and far from apathy and mediocrity. When you fast and pray you are effectively being sharpened to the word of God in your spirit, your conscience and your moral compass. Now you have become a powerful weapon in the hand of God — a razor-sharp edge that is able to slash the enemy when you speak.

A mentor once taught me: "Anything that is cutting-edge must be narrow by necessity." When we fast and pray, we are being sharpened and narrowed for effectiveness to destroy the powers of darkness and advance the kingdom of our God. The Holy Spirit wants you and I sharp and effective so our integrity can be enduring.

"For the word of God is living and powerful, and sharper than any two edged sword, piercing even to the division of soul and spirit, and of joints and marrow, and is it discerner of the thoughts and intents of the heart."
Hebrews 4:12

Integrity and honor is a lifestyle. It's not a seasonal pursuit. It's a life-long continual pursuit for the heart of God and a perpetual life of revival advancing His kingdom in the earth. The pattern Jesus laid out in Matthew chapter six looks like this: He said, "when you give"..."when you pray"..."when you fast." Notice Jesus didn't say "if" you fast.

Ecclesiastes 4:12 says, "...and a threefold cord is not quickly broken." The three fold cord of a believer's lifestyle is giving, praying and fasting. God desires for everyone of us to apprehend breakthroughs and victories in life. Disciplining our lifestyle to God's three-cord pattern will keep us focused and prepared in adversity, challenges and attack.

A lifestyle of prayer and fasting is your secret strength. Jesus said, *"My food is to do the will of Him who sent Me, and to finish His work"* (John 4:34).

I love the interaction of Jesus and his disciples in this chapter. Their appetite was on one frequency and His was tuned into the Father's intensions. Jesus told his disciples He had food to eat that they didn't know about. From what I can tell, after studying deeply the Greek in this passage, Jesus wasn't hiding a Snickers or M&M's in His sash for extended ministry times to hold Himself over. As the disciples were trying to figure out who had brought Him food, He told them the secret - "My food is to do the will of Him who sent Me; and to finish His work." Jesus was drawing strength and nourishment that sustained Him because His mission was to fulfill the Father's desires.

Nothing will nourish our lives like living in the will of God and accomplishing His purposes and desires. The will of God will feed you and sustain you — carrying you forward through any and all circumstances. Like Jesus, we too can tap into the secret resources and find the pleasure of doing the work of our Father will feed us. *"...Man shall not live by bread alone, but by every word that proceeds out of the mouth of God"* (Matthew 4:4).

Intimacy with the Father can build up a storehouse of strength and power that can sustain us and keep us moving forward through any difficult situation, temptation or circumstance. We can draw forth from the intimacy that we share with Father that will feed us and others.

Appetite for Victory
"The tempter came to him and said, "If you are the Son of God, tell these stones to become bread."
Matthew 4:3

Isn't it interesting, that the devil, of all things, tempted Jesus at the end of His fast trying to provoke Him to turn stones into bread? Of course we know that Jesus had the power to do so, however, don't miss this powerful and practical point — Jesus came to use His power to serve others, not Himself. Jesus was determined to finish His fast strong because he had an appetite for victory — our victory.

When Jesus returned from the wilderness in His 40 day fast, He immediately began to do "mighty miracles, healing all who are oppressed by the devil" (Acts 10:38). The enemy was scheming his very best to seduce Jesus to get focused on His own need, because He knew that Jesus was going to receive the power of the Holy Spirit that was going to change and transform the world.

The devil comes with an appetite for destruction only to steal,

BOLD AS LIONS

kill and destroy you. Make no mistake. The devil is after your integrity. Never let him have it. Jesus had an appetite for complete victory. He was looking ahead knowing His breakthrough would become our breakthrough and His triumph would become our triumph. I have learned, and I continue to learn, that our personal breakthroughs are not just about us. In God's wisdom, they are always connected to others. In fact, the anointing on our lives is not just for us, but it has always been about others being set free.

Perhaps one of the most profound characteristics about the resurrection power of God is that it has an appetite to bring to life that which is dead. Whatever His Glory touches, it will live. What if His Glory touched your city? Your region? Your marriage? Your dreams? Your finances?

In a lifestyle of prayer and fasting, our appetite for complete victory increases. Can you see yourself flowing in the power of the Holy Spirit helping others to breakthrough into new realms of God's authority over the enemy?

> *"And do not be conformed to this world, but be transformed by the renewing of your mind, that you may prove what is that good and acceptable and perfect will of God."*
> Romans 12:2

A lifestyle of prayer and fasting prepares the way. Fasting is an extraordinary process that helps us to discover and confirm the will of God, for our lives. When you present your body as a "living sacrifice" you open your spirit up to hear the Lord's voice. Throughout many years, my wife and I have experienced time and again through fasting the discovery of the will of God and directional promptings and pieces of the prophetic puzzle for our family and ministry.

In fasting, you will prove and discover his good and perfect will for your life. The Apostle Paul was fasting when God called him and shared his divine assignment for his life (see Acts 9:7-9). The Apostle Peter was fasting in Joppa, sitting on a rooftop when God gave him a new and fresh revelation and called him to take the gospel to the Gentiles (Acts 10). Jesus was fasting forty days before he was launched into the most epic ministry that revealed to us what "on earth as it is in heaven" truly looks like.

INTEGRITY & HONOR

Fasting prepares the way for God to give you strong integrity, fresh revelation, vision and clear purpose. That's what everyone is really hungry for. I have faith that you too will hear the voice of the Lord afresh, and receive direction and guidance. Jesus said, "Ask and it will be given. Seek and you will find. Knock, and the doors will be open" (Matthew 7:7-8).

Examine Yourself
"Examine me, O Lord, and try me; Test my mind and my heart."
Psalm 26:2
"Create in me a pure heart, O God, and renew a steadfast spirit within me."
Psalm 51:10

A lifestyle of prayer and fasting will always lead to integrity and honor. Fasting is a time where we stand before the Lord with integrity and we ask him to examine our hearts, our lives, motives and intentions. In 1 Corinthians 11, the Apostle Paul tells us to make sure we "examine ourselves" before receiving the communion table of the Lord in the bread and the cup.

In Psalm 139, David says, "investigate my life." It is so important that when we pray and fast, we examine ourselves and we invite the Holy Spirit with His purifying fire and cleansing grace to remove anything from our lives that is not pleasing unto the Lord. There can be no passivity for sin. May we all have the courage to pray "investigate my heart" and "investigate my life" and make it clean. Our desire is clean hands and a pure hearts.

What if we decided that all we really want in life is to be a people after God's own heart? A pure heart. A pure pursuit. A pure reward. May this be our legacy

BOLD AS LIONS

Chapter 4

PREVAILING CHURCH
The Ekklessia Of Glory And Victory

*Jesus said, "I will build My church and the gates of hell
will not prevail against it."*
Matthew 16:18

In the creation account that Moses received, God allowed Moses to stand within the cleft of the rock and peer into the glory of God as He passed before him. Moses was allowed to behold God in this unique way that God alone designed. He told Moses that He would cover him with His hand as He passed and that He would remove His hand to behold His back. According to scripture, Moses had talked with The Lord face to face as with a friend; but in this particular encounter, God would not show His face to Moses but His back. In the King James Version it gives us a snippet of comical language which says; that Moses saw God's "hind parts or back parts." Stay with me here…that doesn't mean that God "mooned" Moses with His hind or back end. What this means in the literal Hebrew is that when Moses looked out the from the clef of the rock as God passed by on Mount Sinai, he was given the ability and access to peer into where God had been in eternity past — before time began — and there he was shown something far beyond blu-ray quality - the marvel and wonder of God's great genius in speaking and shaping creation. "In The Beginning, God…" (Exodus 33)

In Genesis 1:26, Moses writes that God said, *"'Let Us make man in Our image, according to Our likeness; let them have dominion over the fish of the sea, over the birds of the air, and over the cattle, over all the earth and over every creeping thing that creeps on the earth. So God created man in His own image; in the image of God He created him; male and female He created them. Then God blessed them, and God said to them, 'Be fruitful and multiply; fill the earth and subdue it; have dominion over the fish of the sea, over the birds of the air, and over every living thing that moves on the earth.'"*

Notice from the beginning, only mankind was created in the likeness and image of our Creator God. This was His dream and design. This means we have His nature. We also learn that within God's blessing upon mankind is the commission and function of leadership and dominion. This role is inherent in our nature and is fundamental to our design and our destiny.

The scriptures and creation reveal to us that God is Sovereign; possessing supreme and ultimate power. God is Omnipotent - meaning that He is all-powerful. God is Omnipresent; meaning He is everywhere. God is Omniscient; meaning that He is all knowing and He is the Supreme Ruler. Psalm 103:19 says, *"The Lord has established His throne in heaven, and His kingdom rules over all."* Colossians 1:16, says, *"For by Him all things were created that are in heaven and that are on earth, visible and invisible, whether thrones or dominions or principalities or powers. All things were created through Him and for Him."* Psalm 24:1 says, *"The earth is the Lord's, and all its fullness, the world and those who dwell therein."* Psalm 115:16 says, *"The heaven, even the heavens, are the Lord's; but the earth He has given to the children of men."* Don't miss this; the *earth* He has given to the children of men. Notice this design of delegated authority and dominion that the Lord has given to His ultimate creation — mankind — those created in His own image are given the responsibility to steward the earth and walk in our inherent destiny.

Under man's delegated authority, the earth would be blessed because man and woman were blessed by our Creator and loving Father. The idea of the condition of the earth being directly related to the condition of mankind is reinforced by the fact that when Adam and Eve sinned, both man and the earth were placed under a curse. Through the sacrificial Lamb of God and the profound glory of His cross, Jesus was cursed by our sins. The gospel reveals that this curse of sin was broken off of mankind at the crucifixion. Galatians 3:13 says, *"Christ has redeemed us from the curse of the law by becoming a curse for us, because it is written; everyone who is hung on a tree is cursed."* Second Corinthians 5:21 says, *"For he made him who knew no sin to be sin for us, that we might become the righteousness of God in him."* God pronounced His blessing upon us in the beginning. He commissioned us with an assignment of dominion; and through the cross that Jesus willingly paid for us, he redeemed and ransomed us; restoring us and re-commissioning us — to the original design of union with the Father. The design of *on earth as it is in heaven*.

When Jesus asked His disciples, *"Who do men say that I am?* He was not insecure about who He was. He was never questioning His identity. He was looking for revelation. Peter responded to him, *"You are the Christ, the son of the living God."* Jesus told him that His Father in heaven had revealed this to Peter. It was upon this rock of revelation He would build His Church, and the gates of hell will not prevail against it.

In Matthew 16:19, Jesus says, *"And I will give you the keys of the kingdom of heaven, and whatever you bind on earth will be bound in heaven, and whatever you lose on earth will be loosed in heaven."* The Williams Bible Translation says, *"I solemnly say to you, whatever you forbid on earth must already be forbidden in heaven, and whatever you permit on earth must already be permitted in heaven."*

We have keys to unleash heaven on earth and keys to forbid the powers of darkness. I want us to recognize the divine partnership that we share with the Holy Spirit to create the Father's design; on earth as it is in heaven. When we look at Matthew chapter six, Jesus gave this epic prayer to his disciples that it was His Father's will for life on earth to be just as it is in heaven. Truly the kingdom of God would come to earth and God's will would be done.

The Question is: Who Is In Control & Who is In Charge?

When you look at Jesus and read the Gospels, you find out that the will of God is not complicated or hard to understand. It is no secret that the subject of the will of God has been debated long and hard.

BOLD AS LIONS

There are two different words used in the original language of the New Testament for the *will* of God. The first word is *boulema* and the second is *thelema*. *Boulema* is the word that reveals the will of God as to what is firmly established and settled in the will of God. In *boulema*, this will of the Lord happens regardless of who believes it, endorses it or opposes it. The return of Christ falls into this category of the will of God. The word *thelema* is much different as it refers to the will of God as God's desires, intentions or wishes. For example, God is not willing that any should perish (2 Peter 3:9). Yet people are perishing everyday. This will of God's is obviously dependent upon people's response to God's heart — those who are hearing the Gospel and by those who are commissioned by God to carry the good news of the kingdom to the ends of the earth. We have a responsibility in this part of God's will being accomplished.

This is huge. God has dreams and desires that may or may not be fulfilled based upon how we respond to the Holy Spirit's inspiration. Think deeply about that. Make no mistake, God has the power to make anything happen that he wants to happen, but His heart's desire is to patiently develop us so that we yield to His word, take responsibility and co-labor with Him. The outcome of this process is we become the people who look and live just like Jesus, accomplishing the will of God in the earth.

The first word for the will of God, *boulema*, refers to the things that are unchangeable with God. An obvious example of this is the return of Christ. Jesus is coming back, weather people believe it, accept it, mock it or they really don't care. The promise has been given. Jesus said he was going to return and nothing can stop it. According to Jesus, His return was entirely in the hands of the Father, who alone determines how and when this event will happen. On the other hand, there are many things that God would like to have happen and has made possible, but they never will be, because believers either don't believe that it is the will or purpose of God or they are waiting for God Himself to do them. That will is represented in the word *thelema*.

One of the most common phrases used in this discussion on God's will is that "God is in control." As I said before, God is sovereign. He rules overall. Everything belongs to him. There's nothing outside of His reach and care. He is all knowing and all-powerful. But is He in control? I'm certainly not questioning His ability, power and authority.

If He is, doesn't that make Him responsible for ISIS, World Wars I and II? How about sickness and disease? How about starvations and clean water for nations? If He is in control, then He deserves the credit for earthquakes, hurricanes, tornadoes and all the other calamities or acts of nature. I think you're getting the point.

I belive it's more accurate to say that God is in charge, but He's not in control.

The lazy man's theology makes himself responsible for nothing. It always places the responsibility or the blame squarely upon God; because He's in control. When we get to this juncture at the crossroads of the will of God, we actually have to decide who is in control here. Who did Jesus give authority to? Who did He give his power and presence to deal with every kind of threat, crisis, tragedy, demon or disease. He gave it to you and me.

Everybody knows that God can make any situation turn around for His glory. God is amazingly that good, and I for one, am extremely thankful for that. I have witnessed very difficult things that have happened to people that love and serve God. I've also seen the intervention of God's grace turn it around, healing hearts and restoring lives to unexplainable victory. But when we credit God to being in control and credit Him with the cause of problems, disease and chaos it is simply far beyond being irresponsible. It violates and misrepresents His very character, essence and nature.

Before Jesus ascended into heaven on the Mount of Olives, the apostle Matthew writes that Jesus spoke to them saying, *"All authority has been given to me in heaven and on earth. Go therefore and make disciples of all nations, baptizing them in the name of the Father and of the Son and of the Holy Spirit, teaching them to observe all things that I have commanded you; and low, I am with you always, even to the end of the age. Amen"* (Matthew 28:18-20).

God has given you and I authorization in the earth, authority and power for dominion. As sons and daughters of God, we have been given a global commission to deal with natural and spiritual matters. So often we are asking God to deal with things that, quite frankly, He expects us to deal with because He has already given us the authority and the power. God has given us revelation, wisdom, counsel and insight through His word and unprecedented power by the Holy Spirit. It is our responsibility to treasure it, believe it, walk in it, establish it and speak it out. Then we will see the kingdom expand.

At this point in history, as we look at life here on planet earth we should be asking some deep probing questions. Perhaps you're thinking and wondering, why is there so much chaos in the world and where is God in all this? Where is the Church? More to the point, where is the Church that the gates of hell are not prevailing over? It is not in my heart to be provocative in any way, but to be truthful, so that we move in revelation rather than ignorance. You've heard the old preverbal phrase, "Ignorance is bliss." Well, it's not. Ignorance is destroying purpose, design and destiny. The scripture tells us plainly, "My people are destroyed for lack of knowledge…" (Hosea 4:6).

Many well meaning Christians say, "God is in control," yet the Scriptures teach something much different than that. I referenced above to Psalm 115:16, *"The heaven, even the heavens are the Lord's; but the earth He has given to the children of men."* When it comes to the order of nature (the sun, the moon, the stars, the cosmos, and planets) I have to agree. Look at the nature of ecosystems (plants and trees and animals). The seed bearing process continues just as the earth remains in seedtime and harvest. You can't help but see God's brilliant design. The order that God has structured is flawless and perfect in every way. "The sun will come up tomorrow. Bet your bottom dollar that tomorrow — there'll be sun!" Thanks Annie. God is most certainly in "boulema". He has set the oceans in their place, establishing their boundaries. He has hung the celestial infrastructure of planets perfectly in orbit, spinning like tops in the light of the burning sun.

However, when it comes to *mankind*...

"Houston, we have a problem!"

Stay with me here.

Look at our world. If God was in control, what would it look like here on the earth? I submit to you, if God was in control, it would look just like heaven. But the earth has been given over to the sons of men. Presently, the earth does not look like heaven and that's why Jesus told us to pray, "Your kingdom come, Your will be done on earth as it is in heaven." We received a blessing — the commission of dominion — and that is our responsibility.

I submit to you that God is *not in control*. However, He is most certainly in charge. He has always been in charge and will always be in charge. He's the Sovereign Almighty God of heaven and earth. God is in *charge,* meaning that He is Sovereign and has supreme power over all things.

Parents understand this control issue all too well. They learn quickly who's in charge and who is in control. As a father or as a mother, you have ultimate authority and oversight, and you are in charge of your home. As a father of two teenagers, and married for more than 22 years, I can tell you I have never been in control of my house. You may be laughing now. Or maybe you're mad at me because I just told you God is not in control. I'm not in control of my house. I'm called to be in control of my own life. Things have happened and continue to happen in our home that are completely out of my control. Daily? Yes. Weekly? Yes. Monthly? Yes. Yearly? Yes. It doesn't take that long to understand the revelation that I am not in control of others. You cannot control your children and you cannot control other people. It's lofty and arrogant to think we can. The truth is, we cannot control others and God does not control. A friend of mine likes to say, "On a good day you're able to control yourself." He's right. That's the fruit of the Spirit: self-control. What I have learned as a father is that I am in *charge*. When the rules and boundaries of our family culture have been broken, dishonored or mismanaged, my children are brought to me because I'm their father. Fathers and mothers are called to bring order, instruction, discipline and correction. I don't operate in this function because I'm in control, it's because I'm in charge. Do you see the difference?

Is God in control of you, or are you learning to surrender your will to him in love? Is God in control of you, or are you starting to awaken to the mystery that your life is a special treasure to the Creator that is Sovereign and in charge? Is God controlling you or are you learning that trust and obedience is beautiful to Him?

I had a mentor in my life tell me many years ago to be careful in leading people. He said, "Some people would rather be controlled than trusted. The reason they would rather be controlled is if things don't work out the way they expect or anticipate they can come back and place the blame on you. However, if you trust them in their own path, and it doesn't work out, the blame rests upon them."

Would you rather be controlled or trusted? God has invested an enormous amount of trust in you and me.

BOLD AS LIONS

God is not a control freak, never has been, never will be. This may be hard for us to get our mind around, but God wasn't even in control in heaven when His own angelic creation (in eternity past before time began) fell, seduced by Lucifer as he was lifted up in his pride and iniquity was exposed in him. He was judged as the one who lusted to be equal to and worshipped as God Almighty. The scriptures tell us that 1/3 of the angelic hosts were banished, cast out of heaven for their rebellion with Satan. Jesus said, that he saw Satan fall like a bolt of lightning from heaven. Was God in control? No. Was God fully in charge? Yes, absolutely. You see the difference? God is love and love does not control, it doesn't seek its own. Love gives perfect freedom and liberty. The kingdom is not a free-for-all, it's a kingdom of honor and divine order and justice. In His sovereign love and authority, God reveals that He is all-powerful and fully in charge (see Ezekiel 28).

While we are on this subject, I just want to make a special note concerning this epic transition from eternity past. Many times, you hear preachers exaggerating grandiose descriptions of the celestial conflict in heaven when Lucifer was cast out of God's presence to the earth. 1 John 1:5, tells us that, *"God is light; in him there is no darkness at all."* The truth is, this was not some massive fight in heaven. When God recognized that Lucifer's thought had become his intention, it was then that iniquity was revealed within him. This "war" in heaven perhaps lasted a nanosecond. Lucifer didn't rally a third of his angels with swords and shields drawn to take the Throne. There was no real "war". God wasn't anxious and white-knuckling His throne. He didn't have to call upon the reinforcements of Michael and Gabriel, and his faithful and loyal angels because there was a problem with Lucifer. No, there was no celestial battle or cosmic war in heaven which God was finally able to get under control and sit back down on His throne. The moment that Lucifer shifted into a realm of intent, he was cast out of the glorious light of God into the darkness instantly. The reason is because in God there is only light, and there is no darkness in Him whatsoever. That is why Jesus said, "I saw Satan as lightning fall from heaven." Instantly stripped of his name, his office, his heavenly position. At the speed of light he was cast out of the glory of Almighty God.

What if I told you plainly that Christians like to say that God is in control so that they can remain lazy? Many Christians like to live passively unengaged and irresponsible. There are many Christians that do not like to take ownership or carry their weight of responsibility of the grand commission that God has given us in the earth. They behave as immature sons and daughters. There's really no need to pray because God is in control. We can just coast on autopilot, right? Wrong. I know this is strong, but it's a destructive belief that God is in control of everything that happens upon the earth, and that in His Sovereignty, He always gets what He wants. What a misconception. Think about how many countless people there are right now who are missing out on revival and awakening because of their belief that God is in control; they believe that if God wants to send revival He will simply do it. If you believe this in your theology, then all of these people are not being saved simply because God didn't choose to do so. Think about that…are you thinking?

Satan is trying to occupy a dominion he no longer rightfully owns. Many chose to simply throw up their hands and say God is in control. I have to question that. All you have to do is look at this world with over 55+ million babies that have been aborted right here in America since my birth year of 1973, while nations rage with war against other nations, while starvation destroys the destiny of nations, while militant gays and lesbians are taking over and perverting every sector of community, while corruption and wicked leaders are destroying the very fabric of our own nation, while gross immorality and sexual confusion rages for it's demanded rights and self-indulgences. Is God in control? No. If He was in control the earth would reflect heaven. We have broken our design, our blessing, our commission for dominion.

I have to tell you plainly that God is *not in control*. God is *in charge*. He is the holy and righteous Judge. One day all things will return to The Father and He will judge every tribe, tongue and nation on how we honored His heart, and how we managed the authority that He gave us to steward life in the earth. God is looking to you and I, His church, to arise and take responsibility, take action, preach righteousness and bring the kingdom of God right into culture. Some might say that these issues are political and they refuse to go there. Once again, that is because the body of Christ has been extremely lazy and enjoys floundering. Shame on us. We need to have the courage to repent and leave behind our religious platitudes. The kingdom of God was always meant to invade in shaping culture, never to retreat from it.

Kenneth Hagan used to teach years ago about how the church

or individuals can get to a place of disobedience that God can't even help them. One time when he was speaking on this subject a man spoke out in service and said, "I don't believe that! God is sovereign and He is in control and He can make anything or whatever He wishes to happen." Without hesitation, Kenneth Hagan responded, "If God is in control then why can't He make you give your tithes?" The man shut his mouth and slid down his chair.

While many are praying, "Lord, come down" - the good news is that He already has come down in the flesh. John 1:14 says, *"The Word became flesh and dwelt among us, and we beheld His glory, the glory as of the only begotten of the Father, full of grace and truth."* Do we recognize what was freely given in Jesus — that love has come down and He has given us the kingdom? While many are praying, "Lord, rend the heavens, open the heavens," He already has. Luke chapter three, tells us that at Jesus's baptism in the Jordan River, the heavens opened — literally meaning "torn apart" (just like the veil in the tabernacle) as the Holy Spirit descended upon Jesus. The heavens are open. While we are praying for the Lord deal with the principalities and the ruling governing spirits over our regions, the Scriptures tell us plainly in Colossians 2:15, *"... Having disarmed principalities and powers, he made a public spectacle of them triumphing over them in it."* We have been raised with Christ and seated in heavenly places to function from the place of unprecedented victory (Ephesians 1&2). We are not under circumstances, nor under a cloud of demonic rule, or power on this earth. We have been immeasurably blessed by our Father, re-commissioned and given the authority of our victorious Lion of Judah.

It is imperative right now that the church repents and dismisses the religious, poverty and powerless mentality. We must have an awakening that the church is on the offense not on the defense, and that we are here to transform the world because God has placed us in control. And from this place of victory we must recognize we have great authority to expand the kingdom so that the knowledge of the glory of the Lord covers the earth even as the waters cover the sea. We have been commissioned as ambassadors of the King of kings and Lord of lords.

In Luke 9:2, it says, *"Then he called his twelve disciples together, and gave them power and authority over all devils, and to cure diseases. And he sent them to preach the kingdom of God. And to heal the sick."* This is

PREVAILING CHURCH

an extraordinary picture of what dominion looks like. Jesus gave us a gospel that can be demonstrated with power, signs and wonders. Far too many believers are content with maintaining prayers that say — "God, I want you to do this for me", "God, go ahead and please do this"…instead of saying, "God, you have blessed me and you have placed me here, and now by your great grace use me. Use me and I will partner with the Holy Spirit. Let's do this together." Remember, *"The heaven, even the heavens, are the Lord's; but the earth he is given to the children of men."*

There is a reason that the earth is remaining in a famine of real leadership. The reason is because the church has forsaken its responsibility as sons and daughters. We need to know our identity and our assignment. We need to know who is really in control. Those who know the glory and majesty of Christ and their identity and authority as sons and daughters of God will be those who fulfill the extraordinary prophetic unveiling of Romans chapter eight — *the sons of God being manifested in the earth so that creation itself is delivered from its bondage and corruption into the glorious liberty of the sons of God* (see Romans 8).

In this hour, it is no time to be casual. It is a time to be courageous. We must recognize that God has placed the church to serve and transform our cities, and disciple nations. Make no mistake about it; all things will go back to our Father because He is in charge. He rules and reigns and is enthroned in glory. We will all give an account unto Him as His children because He is the Sovereign God. We have so much to accomplish, and so much work must be done.

The Church That Jesus Is Building

"When Jesus came into the region of Caesarea Philippi, He asked His disciples, saying, "Who do men say that I, the Son of Man, am?" So they said, "Some say John the Baptist, some Elijah, and others Jeremiah or one of the prophets." He said to them, "But who do you say that I am?" Simon Peter answered and said, "You are the Christ, the Son of the living God." Jesus answered and said to him, "Blessed are you, Simon Bar-Jonah, for flesh and blood has not revealed this to you, but My Father who is in heaven. And I also say to you that you are Peter, and on this rock I will build My church, and the gates of Hades shall not

BOLD AS LIONS

> *prevail against it. And I will give you the keys of the kingdom of heaven, and whatever you bind on earth will be bound in heaven, and whatever you loose on earth will be loosed in heaven."*
> (Mathew 16:13-19)

The disciples' answer to the question was imperative. Jesus really didn't care about his poll numbers and He surely wasn't confused about His identity. He was seeking their level of revelation. After hearing their response, Jesus pointedly asked them, "Who do you say that I am?" Peter answered, "You are the Christ, the son of the living God." The Scriptures are full of these transformational and transcendent moments where there is a massive unfolding and collision of eternal revelation into time. One of them is when Abraham is on Mt. Mariah ready to offer his own promised son. Moses was at a burning bush, receiving a commission to deliver a nation in bondage. David was facing a giant with nothing but a sling in his hand and a burning heart for God. Peter experienced this burst of spiritual clarity and recognized who had transcended into time. This was not just another skilled and wise rabbi. This was not just a prophetic messenger. No. The answer was profoundly revelatory and earthshaking. Jesus answered Peter and told him that he was blessed because flesh and blood did not reveal it to him but the Father in heaven.

Jesus said, "Upon this rock I will build my Church and the gates of hell will not prevail against it." This word, "church" is the greek word *ekklesia*. Its meaning is something far different than the English word "church" or what we have come to know in our present church culture. I have pioneered and pastored two different churches and ministered in hundreds of churches throughout America and other nations. This is not what Jesus was talking about. The church produces one thing and the ekklesia produces something far greater. The intentions of Jesus were to give birth to the ekklesia. The language of Matthew 16 is actually a watershed moment of divine revelation. This is actually a turning point in the message of Jesus which becomes a cornerstone that gives birth to a kingdom culture. This "rock" that Jesus said his church will be built upon is none other than the rock of ages — Christ himself.

For the disciples, they understood ekklesia in their culture to mean an assembly of people to govern the affairs of a city, state or

PREVAILING CHURCH

nation as in a parliament or congress. In the Roman culture, it was an assembly of people sent into a conquered region to govern and atler the culture until it reflected Rome. The ekklesia infiltrated government, social culture, language, the arts, education, ect., until the people structured their thoughts, actions and way of life like the Romans. In other words, the ekklesia assignment was to install the culture and ideas of the Roman kingdom. This is epic, because when Jesus said He would build His church — His ekklessia — He was announcing a body of people that would legislate spiritually for Him to extend His Kingdom government and influence on the earth.

On this "rock" He said He will build His ekklesia, His Father's house *would be a house of prayer for all nations*. This church is a radiant, bold and ruling church, with power and authority over the forces of darkness. The ekklesia is the covenant keeping sons and daughters who know how to model and release the authority of Christ in the earth.

In biblical days, the ekklesia was the elders, social watchmen and those who governed the affairs of what a culture would permit or would not permit among their towns and villages. They were the ones that set the agenda for what was allowed and what would be acceptable amongst their people. The ekklesia met at the gates of the community to legislate and give authorization to a life-giving community. It is a strong prophetic revelation of where the true church is set in place to give access or closure. This declaration from Jesus is an extraordinary leap as we begin to tap into the revelation of the destiny, authority and dominion of our purpose in bringing the will of God into every sphere of society. Jesus has commissioned us as His ambassadors and has given us the privilege to design earth to reflect heaven's culture. This was the father's desire from the beginning and this is why He gave Jesus authorization to teach us to pray, "Your kingdom come, Your will be done, on earth as it is in heaven."

The ekklesia by definition was a governmental assembly. Its authority and function was to fundamentally bring forth what Jesus inaugurated in Matthew 16:18. This ekklesia (the church) were those that the gates of hell would never prevail against. The ekklesia are the ones who shoulder the responsibilities as representatives of God's ruling council in the earth. Christ remains as the Head (see Ephesians 5:23) and His Body remains in the earth from generation to generation, expanding the rule and habitation of the kingdom.

BOLD AS LIONS

According to Jesus, the ekklesia would be a threat to every corrupt human government and principality. The disciples understood this. But that's frankly not good enough. We are the ones in 2018 who must understand it. We must have a revelation and understanding like never before if we're going to take this position and begin to move into our divine assignments. In His great commission, Jesus said that all authority has been given to Him which was in heaven and on earth (Matthew 28). He told us to go and make disciples of all nations, and that signs and wonders would follow us, and accompanying those who believe. He told us that in His name we would cast out demons and speak with new tongues. He told us we would exercise authority as the true church in power and victory (Mark 16).

The Expansion of the Kingdom

The ekklesia recognizes first and foremost that Jesus holds all authority. Demonized systems cannot defeat them because the church have been given the keys in which they forbid and permit localities on the earth. The ekklesia is a living embodiment of Christ on the earth — His Body. The ekklesia represents His role in the earth. In Joel chapter 2, the church intervenes as the intercessory arbiters of national crisis.

Right now, the church is going through a massive transformation, and it comes through revelation of understanding our identity as His ekklesia. It is not enough to be a good healthy church that can evangelize, feed the poor, build the family and run excellent children programs. Are these important? Absolutely, but it's going to take an ekklesia acting with spiritual authority across a region to release transformational power. That is why the ekklesia is founded on apostles and prophets (Ephesians 1:22, 23, 2:20.) The mindset of sent ones and visionaries are far different than pastors and teachers. They are all equally important, however, the chief concern of heaven coming to earth has to be rightly prioritized. The ekklesia are the ones who build God's seat of authority — his throne — in a city and region.

Jesus said in Mark 11:17, *"My house shall be called a house of prayer for all nations."* Prayer is the key power source of ekklesia. Prayer is the way to strategically and accurately legislate for change and transformation. This is where we see the strongholds of murder, drugs, sex trafficking, and new age cultic worship forbidden in our communities. This is where we see abortion being abolished in America because the ekklesia is taking action and moving in power. Prayer is the power of God. Prayer is the front line for the bold and courageous ekklesia, and there can be no retreat.

Jesus said, "...the gates of hell shall not prevail against his church." Gates are the access point. Gates are the places that transition us into something or out of something. The gate is both an exit and an entry. In biblical times, the elders sat in the gates. This is highly symbolic and prophetic for us. I think it's so notable that the promise of dominion over the enemy's gate was declared from the beginning over God's covenant people. In Genesis 22:17, God told Abraham, *"Indeed I will greatly bless you… And your seed shall possess the gate of your enemies."* Galatians 3:29 shouts to us this promise too, *"If you belong to Christ then you are Abraham's offspring, heirs according to promise."* The righteous are as bold as a lion and the righteous ekklesia is going to have to learn how to cooperate and participate in the Spirit to bring the kingdom to our cities, to our nation and to the nations of the earth.

Why is all of this so important? Because it is imperative that the ekklesia takes its stand now. We have been losing far too many battles for the soul of our nation. It's no secret that the assault on marriage has been unprecedented. Legislation is continually drafted in the halls of human power, crafting clever hate speech laws demanding the proclamation of biblical truth illegal. The spirit of lawlessness is being codified in the law and defended in our courts. Perversion and the occult are raging. A radical homosexual agenda, founded by some of the wealthiest men in the world, is demanding that the governments of the earth openly support their cause. What is perhaps most shocking of all, is that governments are bowing to these insane threats. Waves of economic crisis stir hysteria, forcing the fearful masses to forfeit their own authority and independence to the state, in exchange for security and protection. Don't believe it? Just look at Sweden right now.

The death culture of human trafficking, abortion, drug violence and gang wars are all around us. The infrastructures of our cities are crumbling, and the churches remain half empty and satisfied with the status quo. I have to be honest; sometimes I just shake my head bewildered with the condition of the American church at large. We live in an age of gross darkness, among those who call evil good and good evil (Isaiah 5:20). Where is the church? Many feel powerless to respond. Most church people think they've done the world a favor just by being sweet, polite and domesticated saints.

The church that Jesus is building is far superior than just a campus that is used a few days a week, serves coffee and offers modern services. His church is the ekklesia which is the embassy of heaven that builds His throne — His seat of authority — expanding and reaching into every sphere of culture in the unstoppable power of the Spirit. The church that Jesus is building is a burning apostolic force, undefeatable and unquenchable, triumphing over all the works of the devil.

Heaven's agenda cannot continue to be stalled across the nations of the earth because of a sleeping church and a lack of revelation. The demonic culture cannot continue to be permitted its place prevailing in the earth. The church has to begin legislating the kingdom in the place of prayer. Somebody has to wake up. For the most part, the church has been hiding away, safely nestled in their passivity, feeding on inspirational "Ted Talks." Outside of the faithful and passionate remnant, there has been little fire in their souls, and there has been very little intercession for the nations.

I'm here as a messenger to tell you that God's ekklesia, the burning ones, the elders, the gatekeepers and the watchmen (those who know their God) will live in the furnace of prayer, positioning themselves for the awakening and revival beyond anything we have ever conceptually imagined. Our revelation is most crucial. We must behold the Christ who has all authority! I want to ask you plainly, do you see Jesus as having all authority? If you do not, it's time to set everything aside, get away with the Lord and courageously gaze into the fiery eyes of the Lion.

> *"The LORD will go forth like a warrior, He will arouse His zeal like a man of war. He will utter a shout, Yes, He will raise a war cry. He will prevail against His enemies."*
> Isaiah 42:13 NASB

The Holy Spirit is summoning us to assemble together with eternal purpose and focus on the real agenda of bringing the government of heaven into the earth. Our gatherings are destined to become the most exhilarating and powerful gatherings on the face of the earth. The ekklesia will not be wasting away in some lifeless structure of religion. No! They will be accessing the power of the throne of God through earthshaking worship, prayer and intercession. The power of the Holy Spirit will be on radical display. The groans of our world, that are presently under the weight of evil, will be met with the church of power and great glory, bringing deliverance and liberty to the captives. The gates of hell cannot prevail against the revelation of the risen living Christ and His victorious Church!

BOLD AS LIONS

Chapter 5

STEWARDING THE FUTURE
His Manifest Presence

*"On that day I will raise up The tabernacle of David, which has fallen down,
And repair its damages; I will raise up its ruins,
And rebuild it as in the days of old…"*
Amos 9:11

There's nothing like sitting in the hills of Jerusalem. Earlier this year, I was in Israel for two weeks of ministry. It was an epic journey and I was completely overwhelmed by the love of the Father. If I wasn't crying, I was laughing. And if I wasn't laughing, I was crying. It was such an extraordinary experience. During our trip, I set aside a few days with one of my dear friends to spend some quality time in the old city of David and explore the marvels of Jerusalem.

One afternoon, after touring Hezekiah's tunnel and the archeological excavation of King David's palace, I had some time to just sit quietly in the city of David overlooking the Kidron valley towards the Mount of Olives. I began to imagine what it must have been like when David and his mighty army finally returned to Jerusalem and the priest came bearing the Ark of the Covenant. I imagined how wild the celebration and dancing was in the streets on that day. I could see David bursting with joy — spinning, laughing and worshipping unto the Lord with all the passion and strength he possessed — as the ark

BOLD AS LIONS

was set in its resting place on Zion.

Tears were flowing down my face. I couldn't help but think of the soon coming and return of the Son of David, the King of all kings — our Lord Jesus Christ — to rule and reign from His Holy Throne. On that day, I promise you this, my friends, I will be in the streets of Jerusalem dancing the dance of victory and triumph.

The Vow & A Divine Obsession

Have you ever wondered why God called David a man after his own heart? I want to take you back in time to a story of a young shepherd who was in an epic transition for a destiny that's hard to even fathom. The Prophet Samuel had poured the anointing oil on his head and declared that he would be king. Soon after Goliath's body hit the ground and David severed his head, he would be met with an unrelenting evil. David was now hunted night and day like a criminal in the wilderness as Saul worked hard and long to destroy his life. Saul was beside himself, and raging with jealousy and fear knowing David would one day become king in his place. David would be faced with test after test as the Lord prepared him for the throne.

In Acts chapter thirteen, it says, *"After removing Saul, he made David their king. He testified concerning him: 'I have found David son of Jesse a man after my own heart; he will do everything I want him to do.'"* What was David's secret? What was it about David that God would bless him so much, making him king over Israel? What caused David to stand out?

In Psalm 132, as David is on the run for his life and Saul is evolving into a madman, we discover a vow that was made between the heart of David to the heart of God. *"Lord, remember David and all his afflictions; How he swore to the LORD, and vowed to the Mighty One of Jacob. 'Surely I will not go into the chamber of my house, or go up to the comfort of my bed; I will not give sleep to my eyes or slumber to my eyelids, until I find a place for the LORD, a dwelling place for the Mighty One of Jacob.'"* Here we discover David's secret vow and promise to the Lord that was in his heart.

I want to show you an additional scripture that Ezra wrote concerning David's own words. *"However the Lord God of Israel chose me above all the house of my father to be king over Israel forever, for He has* chosen Judah to be the ruler. And of the house of Judah, the house of my father, and among the sons of my father, He was pleased with me to make me king over all Israel" (1 Chronicles 28:4). In the King James version it brings out these special words, "God liked me." "Howbeit the Lord God of Israel chose me before all the house of my father to be king over Israel for ever: for he hath chosen Judah to be the ruler; and of the house of Judah, the house of my father; and among the sons of my father he liked me to make me king over all Israel..." Did you catch that? David said that *God liked him.* I think it would be important for us to know why God "liked" David and was pleased with him.

I believe David was set apart because he was able to get a hold of something that was of the utmost importance to God. He got a hold of a divine thought and a divine objective that was in the mind and heart of the God.

In Psalm 132:5 we read, *"I will not give sleep to my eyes or slumber to my eyelids, until I find a place for the Lord, a dwelling place for the Mighty One of Jacob."* In verse 8 we read, *"Arise, O Lord, to Your resting place, You and the ark of Your strength. Let Your priests be clothed with righteousness, and let Your saints shout for joy."*

In Verses 13-15 we read, *"For the Lord has chosen Zion; He has desired it for His dwelling place: "This is My resting place forever; Here I will dwell, for I have desired it. I will abundantly bless her provision; I will satisfy her poor with bread. I will also clothe her priests with salvation, And her saints shall shout aloud for joy. There I will make the horn of David grow; I will prepare a lamp for My Anointed. His enemies I will clothe with shame, but upon Himself His crown shall flourish."*

Do you see it? David apprehended a divine thought — a divine objective that was God's deepest desire. David was making a promise to God that he would go and find the Ark and restore it back to Jerusalem — to God's chosen mountain of Mt Zion. Here in this Psalm we discover the secret vow that David had made to God, and I submit to you this is the very reason God said, "He is a man after my own heart."

David discovered that God's dream was to be in the midst of His people. In the days of the old covenant, God revealed Himself between the two cherubim on the Ark of the Covenant at the Mercy Seat. The Ark was the Throne of God in the earth, a representation of *on earth as it is in heaven.* When the children of Israel took the ark into battle, Israel

BOLD AS LIONS

was in alignment with God and God gave them unprecedented victory over their enemies.

During Old Testament age, which country was the holiest to God when He looked upon the earth? This is an open book quiz. Right answer — Israel. Which city was the holiest place in Israel? Jerusalem. Which mountain was the holiest place in Jerusalem? The Temple Mount — Mt. Zion. What was the most holy centerpiece of the tabernacle? The Ark was the most holy object on the face of the entire earth at that time. It was the centerpiece of God, at the center of the universe and in the center of God's heart.

Remember, in the Old Testament, God said that he would speak to the high priest from between the cherubim, the place called the Mercy Seat. This was the highest seat of authority where mercy was imparted, sin was forgiven and removed as the blood of a unblemished lamb was poured upon the ark on the Day of Atonement. This protocol of worship is the unveiling revelation of Jesus Christ — the centerpiece of God Almighty's heart eternally.

The ark points to the person and finished work of our Lord Jesus Christ. Moses was given the instruction that the ark was to be created of acacia wood and overlaid with gold. Acacia wood is known in Israel as incorruptible wood. This speaks of Jesus' incorruptible humanity. Jesus came in the likeness of sinful flesh as a man, but there was no sin found in him. In the Scriptures, gold speaks of divinity and deity. The wood was overlaid with pure gold — speaking of the person of Jesus — he was completely human but completely God. The lid on the ark was called — "The Mercy Seat." This seat was one large slab of pure gold beaten and hand hammered into shape as a covering. This slab had two cherubim angels at both ends of the Mercy Seat. The Hebrew word is *kapporeth*.

The lid was never to be lifted, and it covered three items inside the ark: The Ten Commandments, Aaron's Rod and a golden pot of Manna. These commandments speak of our rebellion and our inability to keep God's law perfectly. Aaron's Rod was not just an ordinary rod. It was placed overnight before the ark and because of The Presence, it brought forth fresh shoots, branches, fruit and flowers. Do you remember why God did that? Israel was complaining against God's appointment of Aaron as the high priest, so God showed forth this miracle with his rod to identify his favor upon Aaron and that

He was divinely chosen. Aaron's rod speaks of man's rebellion against God's appointed leadership. The golden pot of manna was the third item inside the ark. In Psalm 78, the scripture calls manna "angels' food." While Israel was wandering in the wilderness for forty years, they were fed by manna that fell like snow from the sky. There was no sickness upon them, and yet they complained and called it "worthless bread." The golden pot of manna speaks of man's rebellion against God's provision.

Every item in the ark speaks of our own sin and rebellion against God, but in God's loving grace, He had them placed inside the ark and covered them so they would not be seen — covered with a mercy seat and sealed with the blood of atonement. In doing this, God was saying that He did not want to look at man's sin and rebellion, but he desired His own mercy to triumph over judgment (see James 2:13). He wanted the blood of The Lamb — The Righteous Son — to redeem us in Christ.

"And He Himself is the propitiation for our sins, and not for ours only but also for the whole world. This means Jesus became our sacrifice to divert God's wrath that was meant for us but it went upon him."
1 John 2:2

The word *propitiation* in the Greek is the exact same word for "mercy seat." When the Apostle John said that Jesus is our propitiation, he was saying that Jesus is our Mercy Seat that covers our sin, disobedience and rebellion. That is why it is so dangerous to lift the Mercy Seat. Some of you may remember the 1981 film, "Raiders of The Lost Ark" with Harrison Ford. It's a favorite in our blu-ray collection at the Gibbs' house. The director, Steven Spielberg, took his liberty in the story as the Nazi's lifted the lid of the mercy seat to inquire what was really inside. In the film, suddenly all these grotesque and ghostly spirits were released and turned violent with burning fire annihilating everything that stood before the ark. Spielberg took a director's twist, but the reality was that the mercy seat was never to be lifted at any time and the consequence for doing so were severe. The Bible records that when the men of a village called "Beth Shemesh" lifted the mercy seat to look inside the ark, many of them were struck dead and destroyed (see 1 Samuel 6:19). I have good news for you, God does not see our sins any longer. God's mercy and grace is exalted above the law.

Moses brought us the Law, but Jesus brought us grace and truth (see John 1:17).

Zion — God's Resting Place

David said, *"For the LORD has chosen Zion; He has desired it for His dwelling place: 'This is My resting place forever; Here I will dwell, for I have desired it.'"* Why did God choose Zion for His resting place and not Sinai? Mount Zion represents mercy and grace. Mount Sinai represents the law. On the first Pentecost, fifty days after Passover, God gave Moses the Ten Commandments on Mount Sinai. On that day, Israel was found at the base of Sinai worshipping a golden calf and consequently, three thousand people died. On the day of Pentecost, after Jesus' resurrection, God poured out the Holy Spirit on Mount Zion, and 3,000 people were saved. Why? The law or letter kills but the Spirit gives life. The law condemns, but grace bring salvation. Some people portray God as one whose anger endures forever and His mercy is just for a moment, but that is not the gospel. His anger was fully exhausted on the Cross that Jesus bore for you and for me. His judgment upon Jesus reveals His grace to us. It's overwhelming. This is a love that is not of this world. The One *who knew no sin, literally became sin and a curse for us that we might become the very righteousness of God in Christ Jesus* (see 2 Corinthians 5:21). That is mercy, my Friends.

David had a secret vow. He had a divine assignment to bring the ark back to Jerusalem. More than twenty years under Saul's reign, the ark had been in a place called Kirjath Jearim — the place of the woods. Isn't it amazing that it was never in the heart of Saul to go and get the ark, and bring it back to Jerusalem? David grew up in Bethlehem, the same city Jesus was born in. David had grown up learning about the ark and a divine thought, a divine object became his obsession.

When we understand the revelation of the ark, we begin to understand that David desired the Mercy Seat. This is prophetically Christ giving place to the Throne of God's grace and mercy, to shine forth from Zion once again. This is the Gospel.

David was a man after the heart of God. Even though he was a man of war and great bloodshed, he longed for grace and mercy. Grace was in David's core and most evident in that he refused to touch King Saul. This revelation of grace and mercy had so begun to do a work in his own heart, that he refused to kill Saul. The new covenant of grace was at work in a man living in an old and inferior covenant.

Unbroken Focus & Unbridled Worship

Once the ark of the covenant made its way from Kirjath Jearim to Mount Zion, David constructed a very humble makeshift tabernacle. The ark and the burning flame of God's glory resting upon the mercy seat became a rallying point for continual worship. A mentor in my life used to say, "Where there is a throne there will be worship, and where there is worship there will be a throne."

David encircled God's burning presence with worshippers to minister day and night, and night and day. Twenty-four hours a day, seven days a week, three hundred and sixty-five days a year and estimated at least thirty-three years of continual worship unto God. This is another prophetic testimony and picture, speaking of Jesus, walking on the earth for thirty-three years in the glory as the perfection of worship and communion unto God the Father.

David received the baton and inheritance of the continual burning Presence from Moses' tabernacle, which was a copy or shadow of the heavenly tabernacle (see Hebrews 8:5). Leviticus 6:13 says, *"A fire shall always be burning on the altar; it shall never go out."* In Leviticus 6:9, it says, *"...the burnt offering shall be on the hearth upon the altar all night until morning, and the fire on the altar shall be kept burning on it."* Day and night, night and day the fire was burning and the fire never sleeps. David's legacy would not only be the sacrificial offerings of animals, but the sacrifices of pure praise and worship around the Glory.

Jerusalem is a city of seven hills. Sound carries in the most awesome way in the City. When you sit in Jerusalem in the old City of David and clap your hands, the echo of sound reverberates through the Kidron Valley like it's being amplified. It goes on and on. I've done it. Try to imagine the sound coming up out of Jerusalem (psalms, harps, flutes, timbrels, stringed instruments, cymbals, trumpets) filling the open heavens night and day, day and night unto God, around the ark of the covenant. The fire of worship would never sleep. *"Let everything that has breath Praise The Lord"* (Psalm 150).

David had set a vision into momentum that looked like "on earth as it is in heaven," continual worship before the Throne unto the Lord

Almighty. David appointed certain Levites to minister before the ark. In 1 Chronicles 16 and Psalm 134, it says that David hired 4,000 Levite musicians and 288 Levite singers to minister unto God non-stop. That is an epic vision and quite a worship staff. Can you imagine believing for the yearly budget of that staff?

That's quite a different vision from the present day 18 to 22 minutes of structured, mechanical worship in our American services, because we've been told people can't stand and worship that long. You also don't want people to feel awkward or out of place if you linger in worship. We've been told the church model that "really works" is the one that draws the crowds with contemporary worship, fog machines, great lighting and services that gets them in and out within an hour. Get the butts in the seats, motivate, inspire, give announcements, and receive that offering. Beautiful sanctuaries all across the landscape of America and the world are missing what actually matters most — The Glory of The King of Love in our midst.

I'm convinced there's a generation now rising that will refuse the boredom of silly spiritual gymnastics and structures of church culture. In some places, churches have become nothing more than hiding places for faithful saints who pretend like they're making a difference.

Those after God's own heart desire to gaze upon the beauty, wonder and majesty of the Lord in worship and encounter the living God. They hunger and thirst for the Shekinah glory of the Lord. God longs to show up in a way we've never conceptually imagined. I wonder who really wants to host His presence and glory?

The Manifest Presence

My life has been overtaken with a divine obsession. I don't completely understand how the Holy Spirit has so radically possessed my life. All I know is that God has set eternity in my heart, and He has filled me with a vision to steward the future by hosting His manifest presence in the earth.

The Hebrew word translated for "glory" is *kabod*. This word literally means the weightiness or weighty splendor. God is raising the lions, who will be taught the ministry of the Spirit and the art of hosting the Glory and the face of God. There are many throughout the earth that are being set apart for a place of continual burning worship and the habitation of the Glory.

Those who are after God's own heart, must make their own vow to pursue Him at whatever cost, to bring His kingdom into the earth. A dwelling place for the Lord's heart and presence is a place where His raw power can be openly manifested, to bring victory and freedom to multitudes. A habitation is the place of continual burning. Does this describe your passion? Do you yearn for a dwelling place for God in your city? Do you long for a corporate community of friends that are unstoppable in their pursuit to host His presence? What if God wants to use you and your friends to become catalysts or keys, to open wide the gates for the King of Glory?

In Isaiah 22:22 it says, *"I will give him the key to the house of David — the highest position in the royal court. When he opens doors, no one will be able to close them; when he closes doors, no one will be able to open them."* Jesus quoted this prophecy and specifically pointed that this is our inheritance as His Church. Revelation 3:7&8 says, *"...He (Jesus) who has the key of David, He who opens and no one shuts, and shuts and no one opens...I have set before you an open door, and no one can shut it."*

Let me say this very plainly, this is a promise for the people who are after God's heart. When our heart is burning intimately for God to know Him, to seek Him, to worship Him — Jesus releases to us doors to open and shut. What could God do with a corporate community in a city who pursues Him with all their hearts?

I know that the future of the church looks very little like the present wineskin. The roar of heaven is reaching the earth and saying, "Look up here." God is not seeking worship; He seeks worshippers. Worshippers who long to build a throne and seat of authority for Jesus, right in the midst of their city and region. This is a rallying point of unbridled worship and unbroken focus, to become a house of encounter. This is not boring church as we know it, but a dawning of a new renaissance — the sound and song of the Lord. A new sound is going to burst forth, summoning the earth to God's heart and the living Christ. This model of heaven on earth will become the new normal. It will change and transform the atmosphere of entire cities.

To those who long for the Spirit to teach you how to become an atmosphere architect and steward the presence, I say, be courageous. Be bold as a lion. Be willing to forsake the powerless, lifeless barricades and structures of religion.

I have to believe we are on the threshold of breaking past religious conditioning into a whole new dimension. The Holy Spirit longs to show us a more excellent way. I'm so hungry for the glory of the Lord. I'm so hungry for the habitation of His Presence to radically break out in my city and my state. We were born for the outpouring of the Holy Spirit. We were born to host His glorious presence as a habitation in the earth.

I believe the days and years just ahead for the Body of Christ, the corporate expression of how we gather and the intension of our gatherings will be filled with a far-surpassing experience of the tangible glory that we will learn to steward. I believe the church will grow mighty and mature in wisdom, power and strength — learning to bear up under His presence. This will set the stage for the greatest outpouring of the Spirit and awakening the world has even known.

To The Courageous

What if you were able to shape the course of history because of your friendship with God? David did. His friendship with God, and his love for the heart and glory of God shifted heaven and earth. Why don't we let God possess us with a holy unquenchable vision?

If we could just be bold — I mean, really bold — and seek the heart of God for an epic plan to host His presence, I believe we could receive and unleash heaven's wisdom, counsel and power from the Holy Place that will be transformational in the earth. God is calling now for lovers of His heart. Some of you reading this book know that your destiny is to be a rallying point for God's glory in your city and region. Don't compromise from seeking the depths of God heart for this. Pray, fast, and do not relent. Don't settle for religion. Don't waste your life trying to create a place that is just hip, stylish or cutting edge. Who really cares? Frankly, I'm embarrassed with the shallowness of most church culture these days — clouds without rain.

There will be 24/7 houses of burning prayer and worship throughout the earth. There will be "tabernacles of David," houses of encounter, where God puts His kingdom on full display. It's beginning to break forth, and I believe it's going to explode world-wide.

There will places so kissed by God, that truly angels will be ascending and descending upon these gatherings. Why don't we start building a vision that will attract God first, rather than trying to attract people? I believe that if we are courageous enough to consecrate our lives to the Lord and establish the vision to attract the glory of God, the masses may really come. For a cool service? God forbid. For an encounter with God Himself? Absolutely!

The reason we have so little heavenly activity and intervention in our cities is because very few are even praying. They're still fat and satisfied with a religious agenda. I'm hungry to see the Holy Spirit ambush us with heaven's agenda. This is like fire in my soul. I'm not casually writing this book to you. I'm writing page after page in tears, because this is where I live — this is my spiritual address — I have to be a rallying point for heaven. I have to bear witness in my generation that God will tabernacle among us. God is not calling you into a "season" of prayer, intercession and revival. He is calling you and summoning you to a lifestyle and legacy of prayer, worship, power and revival.

The words of A.W. Tozer burn in me. "I want the presence of God Himself, or I don't want anything at all to do with religion...I want all that God has or I don't want any."

Do you believe God longs to show His face to this generation and the generations that are yet to come? May God brand you with a heavenly vision. Someone, somewhere, is going to touch God's heart and it's going to shift his or her city. Someone, somewhere, will be met with the assistance of powerful angel armies to unleash revival and awakening. Someone somewhere, is going to build a team and a family of people who will not quit, who will not relent until heaven comes. Someone, somewhere, there is a leader who will stand in that place for the spiritual destiny of his or her region.

If we can build God's throne with our worship, then what can become possible for us? We have unprecedented access to Him. Now is the time to establish and unleash that seat of authority for God's Mercy Seat to capture our cities. Hey worshipper, I pray that hunger for the presence of God overflows in your heart and soul. I dare you to give your life as a conduit of the manifest presence of God to your generation. If you do, I promise you that God will dedicate Himself to bring you into your destiny, and He will answer with fire from heaven.

The future belongs to those who will be able to bear up under this kind of calling and endure the reproaches that come with it as well.

BOLD AS LIONS

Not everyone will celebrate those who seek this level of pursuit. Do you desire the fullness of God? I have to warn you, David could surely warn you - be ready for the backlash. This journey has great potential to set you at odds with those immersed in the comforts of the ordinary status quo.

Let me quote David, *"For I endure insults for your sake; humiliation is written all over my face. Even my own brothers pretend they don't know me; they treat me like a stranger. Passion for your house has consumed me, and the insults of those who insult you have fallen on me"* (Psalm 69:9).

Those that you love most may write you off. They may shake their heads at you and mock your heart, all because of your zeal for the Presence and the House of God. Nonetheless, I pray that zeal for the Lord's house will consume you like it did David.

The Holy Spirit is ushering in a company of believers all over the earth with this stewardship, this burning zeal, with honor for the dwelling place of God's glory. Those who have pledged their heart and made their vows unto Him will see the fire of Lord that will not be contained to a church campus, but will ignite cities, towns, villages and entire regions. You have been brought into the kingdom for such a time as this, to prepare the way and to host His glory. Be encouraged, you will be part of the most powerful and epic revival the earth has ever seen.

The future belongs to those after God's own heart.

The future belongs to the lion-hearts.

The future belongs to the worshipers, the intercessors, the gatekeepers.

"On that day I will raise up The tabernacle of David, which has fallen down,
And repair its damages; I will raise up its ruins,
And rebuild it as in the days of old…"
Amos 9:11

Chapter 6

INVADING THE DARKNESS
An Epic Commission

"Go into all the world and preach the gospel to every creature..."
Mark 16:15

A mentor in my life had this little one liner that just resonated with me many years ago: "Sameness begets lameness. Lameness begets tameness." For far too long the church has floundered in the sameness of religion and surrendered its raw, wild, primal fire and beauty. Sadly, oh, so sadly, we've become tame, civilized and perhaps worse of all — domesticated.

In C.S Lewis' prophetic classic, "The Lion, The Witch & The Wardrobe," Mr. Beaver and Susan are having a conversation about Aslan — The Lion King.

"Aslan is a lion — the Lion, the Great Lion."

"Ooh" said Susan. "I'd thought he was a man. Is he quite safe? I shall feel rather nervous about meeting a lion"..."

Safe?" said, Mr. Beaver ..."Who said anything about safe? 'Course he isn't safe. But he's good! He's the King, I tell you..."

"He's wild, you know. Not like a tame lion."

Right now, we are in an epic season of change and transformation, where the church is heading into a fresh discovery of our Victorious

Lion — and He is not tame. There's been a lot of religious work put forth to repackage the gospel, and even Jesus, for the sake of relevance in our "post-modern age." You never know what you're going to get. People have images of Jesus looking like a blue-eyed Brad Pitt in a white silk sheets, floating around, blessing people. We've insisted on associating Jesus with a domesticated and civilized faith.

The peaceful, serene and rather sterile atmosphere of the church is about to be energized by the appearing of the untamed Lion in her midst.

Susan was "rather nervous about meeting a lion." I think a lot of ministries across our nation, if they're honest, have feared allowing the untamed Lion access into their domesticated and safe meetings. Church staffs have worked hard at crafting a professional atmosphere, making their services appealing and progressive for the seekers. I think I understand this way of thinking. I don't endorse it, but I think I understand it. Safe services and "safe spaces" have become a cultural flame.

Safe Spaces

"Safe Spaces" are the big deal in this present generation. Some of you may be familiar with this term — Safe Spaces. Originally, safe spaces were created in the LGBTQ community. Their logo is a green circle with an inverted pink triangle in the center. The logo was to show the significance and alliance with gay rights and space that was free from homophobia.

In educational institutions, *safe space* or *positive space* are terms that were originally intended to be used to indicate that a teacher, educational institution, or student body did not tolerate anti-LGBTQ violence, harassment or hate speech. The term *safe space* has since been extended to refer to an autonomous space for individuals who feel marginalized to come together to communicate regarding their experiences. Right now, this has become typical in America's Universities.

Some of you may remember on Inauguration day that OSU (Ohio State University) made headline news because they created *safe spaces* for students to deal with the feelings of anxiety, panic and trauma they were experiencing because of Trumps election. I was in

Washington, D.C. attending and celebrating the historic ceremony of our 45th President. It was a beautiful January morning.

Several months later, I had a powerful dream that I was standing on the football field of the Ohio State Buckeyes. I was surrounded by thousands of students, and there were probably two hundred or more students in front of me, lying on the field flopping violently and erratically, like fish that had been taken out of the pond and thrown ashore. I was walking with a team of ministry friends, who were moving through the students casting demonic spirits out of them. It was a scene of raw power, deliverances and overwhelming salvation in the Holy Spirit. National news outlets were there broadcasting and capturing God's presence. I have to tell you, I have a feeling God's idea of *safe spaces* look much different than what we may expect. When The Lion appears, safe spaces will become a visible unleashing of heaven's power and epic victory on earth. From the Church house, to the White House, to our Universities — We Need The Lion.

Safe Church & Safe Services

We may not like to admit it, but I believe that our perspective and that of God, as to how we function as a Church, are worlds apart. Our gatherings together should be the most exhilarating gatherings here on the face of the earth. The Church is God's chosen anomaly. An anomaly is a "departure from the normal or common order, common form and rule. One that is peculiar, irregular, abnormal, or difficult to classify." There is a generation that is so hungry for the Lion's appearing! There are a lot of people of His presence that are hungry for the Church to become rallying points of supernatural encounter. Rallying points of radical unbridled worship, and dispensers of hope and power. I long to see our generation, by the millions, baptized with The Spirit and with fire. It is no secret that there is an anti-Christ spirit that is working diligently to seduce the people of God. Leaders are especially under attack, deceived into thinking that they must keep the church tame, respectable, and manageable. It's a controlling spirit masquerading as order and wisdom in the church. Unfortunately, it's rooted in the fear of man.

I was ministering in a church a few years ago that was vacillating with their stance at what level they wanted to permit The Lion's presence. They desired a manageable measure of the Holy Spirit. They said they desired "a move of the Spirit — perhaps, revival" but upon further examination it became clear that it was going to be a move of the Spirit on their terms. That church desired the validation of the church's reputation within their city, community and region. As I was ministering there, I saw The Lord in prayer, as The Lion, sitting on the outside looking intensely at the church with unbroken intense focus. It was as if the church wanted The Lion to adhere to their boundaries and to sit outside next to their church signs to attract people to come in, but they didn't want The Lion to walk freely amongst their services. What would they do then? How would The Lion's presence affect their schedule or the "seekers"? Worse yet, how would His presence affect the lukewarm and stale believers?

When the church encounters the revelation of our Lion's splendor, our hearts will burst into fire. His wonder and power will unleash the wild in His sons and daughters. We will discover we were created to run with our Lion King to change the world and invade the darkness with His glory. His power is dangerous and endless love.

The Pride

Cattle move in herds. Birds travel in flocks. Fish swim in schools. Bees move in swarms. Ants move in colonies. I learned recently that in ocean life, whales travel is pods. But when it comes to lions, they travel and live in communities that are called *prides*.

Lions are symbols of strength, fierceness and courage, and have been celebrated throughout history for these characteristics. They are commonly known as symbols of royalty and stateliness, carrying the identity as "king of the jungle". Lions are the only big cats to live in groups called *prides*. Prides are close family groups. They work together to defend territory and hunt.

Our *pride* carries the royal commission to protect and defend our spiritual territory and region, and to stay on the aggressive hunt for the advancement of His glory. The pride is a culture of love, intimacy, passion, loyalty, honor and sacrifice. They are lovers, worshippers, intercessors, watchmen and gatekeepers known for their sacrifice and servanthood. It's here within the pride we discover other lions and lionesses that have covenant hearts who work to build the culture of untamed and radical faith.

The soul of the pride is made alive by the presence of Jesus. Their greatest privilege of all, is learning and moving with the The Lion King Himself. Jesus — the Creator of the universe — identifies Himself with the Lion. He is eternally called the "Lion from The Tribe of Judah" – the heir to David's throne who has won our victory (Revelation 5:5).

As much as religion has tried to tame and domesticate Jesus, He's not tame. He's wild. His love is most fierce — burning with intensity, strength, force, power and aggression. Many have only seen and discovered the attributes of The Lamb in gentleness, kindness and meekness, yet The Lord longs for all to encounter Him as The Lion of fierce, burning, all-powerful and all-consuming love.

Our Lion is triumphant. He is victorious and reigning in great glory and majesty!

If we are going to look into the eyes of The Lion, we need to be prepared for the unexpected. This Lion will break your heart, but in the best way. This is necessary for true friends of the Lion. God told Job, "Brace yourself like a man, because I have some questions for you, and you must answer them." When we look into the eyes of The Lion, He will impart His eternal burning and holy passions, and we need to "brace ourselves" for the impact. Friends of the Lion need their hearts broken and consumed with His desires, dreams and wonders.

It will take great courage to fix our gaze in His eyes. You'll be tempted to turn your head away because your eyes will become rivers of tears. Your heart will be broken and awakened in the depths of your own spirit. Your wells of compassion will burst because suddenly you will see them and hear them. These are the lives, the cries and voices of a lost generation — wandering souls in darkness. You'll smell the stench of social decay and corruption coming up out of our cities. You'll feel the indescribable pain and yearning for our Nation's deliverance from this gross cloud of deception and hopelessness. Your reluctance and resistance to feel this pain and agony of those lost will begin to melt like wax in His presence. The insulation that we built to keep the borders and boundaries from *the world* will come tumbling down. You will hear His roar and tremble at His voice.

Isaiah 66 says, *"Hear the word of the Lord, you who tremble at his word..."* Those who hear the roar of our triumphant Lion will tremble at the sound of His voice.

BOLD AS LIONS

Sometimes, following The Lion can be frightening. Jesus said, *"If anyone desires to come after Me, let him deny himself, and take up his cross, and follow Me"* (Matthew 16:24). The Message Translation reads, *"Anyone who intends to come with me has to let me lead. You're not in the driver's seat, I am. Don't run from suffering; embrace it. Follow me, and I'll show you how."* When you follow The Lion, you deny yourself. This is what true courage is.

An Epic Commission

Moses had to take courage and deny himself. God had heard the cries coming up out of Egypt, and Moses was commissioned back into the devil's playground — the land of slavery, bondage and spiritual darkness — to rescue the children of Israel. Yes, following the Lion can be frightening. Moses would be just one man going into an epic battle against an entire nation. God had plans to transform this struggling man into a hero. He would take a murderer and make him a mighty deliverer. He would transform a shepherd into a courageous prophet and messenger. Moses would go from being a wanderer to a mighty unstoppable leader. How does this happen? Through encountering, trusting and staying with the victorious Lion.

I have good news for you. There is no easy road available for you. What? Yes, you read that correctly. There will be no easy and safe passage in the call of God. It will be dangerous, but that is why The Lion chose to make His home within you. Everywhere the kingdom of God advances, there is a violent engagement against the dark kingdom. Regardless of the cost, the warfare or the sacrifice, we must go. Jesus said, "Foxes have holes and birds of the air have nests, but the Son of Man has nowhere to lay His head." Like Jesus, we too must live according to the agenda of His Father. That's what sets the course for our mission and lifestyle.

I know this is strong, but I need to tell you that none of us who really claim to know and honor Jesus can refuse the path He calls us to walk upon. He promises to lead; you just have to courageously follow and trust the Lion. Jesus will lead you and me into the very heart of the dark kingdom, into the soul of evil, to bear His light and power. We can't go on believing that the life of faith is not a life of risk. He will lead us where mankind has chosen to hide their darkness and shame.

INVADING THE DARKNESS

Just as He sent Moses, He will send you to bring liberty to the captives. Just as the Holy Spirit was upon Jesus, Jesus will commission you.

> *"The Spirit of the Lord is upon Me, Because He has anointed Me*
> *To preach the gospel to the poor; He has sent Me to heal the brokenhearted,*
> *To proclaim liberty to the captives, And recovery of sight to the blind,*
> *To set at liberty those who are oppressed;*
> *To proclaim the acceptable year of the Lord."*
> Luke 4:18,19

Our commission is to invade the darkness and to bring freedom, victory and healing — to loose the captives of our generation. The Holy Spirit desires to breathe upon us to receive His burning obsession. The Holy Spirit desires His lions and lionesses to receive their assignment and carry the torch of His presence into the darkest corners of the earth. The world needs the lions, who come roaring boldly with revelation and experiential truth of The Lion King, speaking the truth in love and bearing the power with it. We don't move forward from a place of mere sympathy, but from a burning authority to conquer the dark kingdom with weapons that are unstoppable.

We haven't been commissioned in our own strength, gifts, talents and abilities. We have been commissioned in the power of The Spirit — the same Spirit that raised Christ from the dead that lives and dwells with you. The Holy Spirit's power is greater than all the armies of the earth combined. If that is so, what are we going to do with it? How will we steward this level of power and authority? What can God do through a man, a woman, a teenager or any individual fully surrendered to the Spirit of God, who will courageously carry the call? Heaven is still seeking and imploring the earth, "Who will go for us?" The Holy Spirit is asking, "Who shall I send? "

> *"For the eyes of the Lord run to and fro throughout the whole earth, to show Himself strong on behalf of those whose heart is loyal to Him."*
> 2 Chronicles 16:9

Jesus said, Go!
"Go into all the world and preach the gospel to every creature. He who believes and is baptized will be saved; but he who does not believe will be

> *condemned. And these signs will follow those who believe: In My name they will cast out demons; they will speak with new tongues; they will take up serpents; and if they drink anything deadly, it will by no means hurt them; they will lay hands on the sick, and they will recover."*
> Mark 16:15-18

Nations are in desperate need of heaven's messengers. Jesus' calling to us is an epic commission. The Holy Spirit is leading His firebrands to invade the darkness. For far too long the church has been stagnating in the culture of comfort and passivity. Far too many leaders have been drunk on the success of meeting their numbers in the seats and offerings. They've settled in. The people lost that primal fire and zeal and went from pioneers to settlers.

In this present move of the Spirit throughout the earth, God is breathing afresh upon those who are drawing near to His heart. They are seeking and finding fresh experiences and encounter in His all consuming love and fire. In that secret place, we are enveloped by God's love — a love that is not of this world — so immeasurable and unfathomable that it transcends human understanding. His dream is that we fall into His embrace and pleasures and cleave unto Him with all our heart and strength.

In this place, we discover His desires and His dream to reconcile all mankind unto Himself. This sacred passion is transferred into our Spirit and made alive. Suddenly, we are awakened to His reality and now our souls are burning in union with His thoughts and intensions. He is an all-consuming fire.

Pioneers & Settlers

This book was written for those who have the blood of explorers and pioneers running through their veins. But it was also written for those who long to establish a pioneering community that will be a sending and mission's station for the future.

When Jesus commissioned His followers, did he call them to be settlers or pioneers? Did he call them to create a fortress of security for the protection of the saints, or did he call them to leave their comfort zone of security far behind? You know the answer; the disciples burst forth as bold pioneers for the expansion of the Kingdom of God.

INVADING THE DARKNESS

Pioneers broke across the frontier of our nation heading west for the expansion of the United States. Pioneers led the way. These forerunners preceded all others exploring and breaking open uncharted territories. They created their own pathway discovering every valley and mountain, crossing every desert and river. The pioneers faced brutal weather and wild animals as they explored the land of opportunity before them. They were adventurers, ready to face danger and even death in their quest of the new frontier.

After the pioneers had broke through they prepared the way for the people we call settlers. When a pathway was created and territories were mapped out, caravans of horse drawn wagons took colonists on a westbound trail looking for a place to establish community and raise families. When these places were discovered, the settlers pitched their tents, and began to build homes and communities.

The settlers built villages, staked out their farmlands, and created settlements. They were willing to defend their new found territory, but had no desire to explore the next valley or climb the next mountain ridge. Settlers preferred safety and security rather than the wild adventure of exploration. That's the difference between pioneers and settlers.

Pioneers are explorers. Deep in their heart they seek to go where no one had gone before. Settlers are different. They seek safety. They avoid risk and prefer the shelter and security.

Follow Him

On a particular day, John the Baptist sent two of his followers to inquire about Jesus' identity and the coming Kingdom. John's disciples asked Jesus, "Are you the one who was to come, or should we expect someone else?" Jesus replied, *"Go back and report to John what you have seen and heard: The blind receive sight, the lame walk, those who have leprosy are cured, the deaf hear, the dead are raised, and the good news is preached to the poor"* (See Matthew 11:3-5). I think it's very notable that Jesus pointed to the miraculous signs of His ministry to confirm to John that Jesus was indeed the Messiah and initiating the arrival of God's Kingdom.

Jesus calls out to His pioneers. His commission is to invade the dark kingdom looks like this. Jesus said, *"And as you go, preach, saying,*

BOLD AS LIONS

'The kingdom of heaven is at hand.' Heal the sick, cleanse the lepers, raise the dead, cast out demons. Freely you have received, freely give" (Matthew 10:7,8).

Freely you have received, now go and freely give. You learn how to give by receiving first. As you are with The Lord receiving of His Spirit, you receive His heart, His burning, His nature and His character.

You learn how to love by having received love. You learn how to give mercy by having received mercy. You learn how to forgive by having received forgiveness. You learn how to give power by having received power. All of these gifts do not come because you had someone significant lay their hand on you in an altar. This comes only from spending quality time with The Lord. When you've received from Him, then out of the overflow you can generously give to all.

If you chose to follow the Lion, and choose to open your heart and give your life for the sake of others, He will unlock your primal spirit, and unleash raw and powerful faith within. How we see Jesus defines how we think and how we live. How we see Jesus determines if we will truly answer the call and if we will be courageous enough to invade the darkness. The way we understand Him will be the way we represent him. Your revelation of who God is to you determines who He becomes through you.

This is our hour. This is our time. This is our watch. Do not underestimate the power of the Holy Spirit within you. Do not set limitations with the natural mind, but renew your mind with the revelation that you are a chosen son and daughter in the kingdom — appointed to bring liberation and victory to this generation. Christ in you is the hope of the nations.

The world is about to encounter and experience the greatest outpouring of the Holy Spirit. He's calling you. He's wooing your heart and soul to be fully set ablaze. You and I are called to be a burning torch in this hour. You are called as His ambassadors and pioneers to bring His salvation, healing and deliverance. Be strong. Be courageous. Be bold as a lion.

(Special Note: In my first book, "Unstoppable & Unquenchable Fire," I explore this level of calling in great detail in chapter three, "Set Your World On Fire" and chapter five, "To The Overcomers.")

Chapter 7

CHAMPIONS
The Rise & Roar of Sons & Daughters

"And it shall come to pass in the last days, says God, That I will pour out of My Spirit on all flesh; Your sons and your daughters shall prophesy, Your young men shall see visions, Your old men shall dream dreams. And on My menservants and on My maidservants, I will pour out My Spirit in those days; And they shall prophesy."
Acts 2:17&18

The Holy Spirit is laying the grounds for a new global awakening in Christianity. From the very beginning of the outpouring at Pentecost in the upper room, the Spirit of God has been igniting sons and daughters with fire, power, prophecy, dreams and vision that are far too compelling to ignore. This Third Great Awakening will surpass anything you and I have ever conceptually imagined possible. God says, He will pour out His Spirit on *all flesh.*

Sons & Daughters
Our Foundation and Identity in The Kingdom

How important is the knowledge of our Sonship and identity? I believe the foundation of our identity for believers is everything. The revelation of Christ in us is one of the most profound and transformational gifts. It is key to victory. However, I also believe that it's not enough to have the understanding of Christ in us. This is not a mental ascent; this has to be experiential and ever-increasing. We must be firmly established in our identity in God as sons and daughters.

Many Christians are engaged in a real battle when it comes to their identity. They deal with an orphan spirit or an orphan mentality — a way of thinking and seeing themselves apart from the family of God. Those engaged in this battle generally struggle with rejection, approval, acceptance, self-worth, value, and esteem. They fight with a sense of belonging or fitting in which leads to a constant need of proving one's self through competitiveness and comparison. The Apostle Paul writes, when we measure and compare ourselves with one another, this is carnal and unwise (see 2 Corinthians 10:12).

In the natural, there are many gifts that we are supposed to receive from a Father that builds a quality life: identity, inheritance, safety and security. In the Jewish culture, when a boy crosses the threshold into a young man they celebrate what is called, "Bar Mitzvah," which means "son of the commandment." Generally, this happens around the age of thirteen where there is a large family celebration. Declarations over the son are given from his father and mother affirming of his identity and coming into manhood (becoming an adult). It's interesting that there's is no biblical account recorded of Jesus' Bar Mitzvah until He enters the waters of the Jordan River to be baptized by John at the age of thirty.

"When He had been baptized, Jesus came up immediately from the water; and behold, the heavens were opened to Him, and He saw the Spirit of God descending like a dove and alighting upon Him. And suddenly a voice came from heaven, saying, "This is My beloved Son, in whom I am well pleased."
Matthew 3:16&17

In this transitional moment, Jesus receives his Bar Mitzvah and declaration by His *Heavenly* Father, "This is my Son, whom, I love and I am well pleased in!" Here we see the proclamation and the gifts of identity, approval, acceptance, value, esteem.

The Apostle Paul writes, *"For you did not receive the spirit of bondage again to fear, but you received the Spirit of adoption by whom we cry out, 'Abba, Father', The Spirit Himself bears witness with our spirit that we are children of God, and if children, then heirs--heirs of God and joint heirs with Christ, if indeed we suffer with Him, that we may also be glorified together"* (Romans 8:15-17).

This is transformational. This is our identity. I think it's very notable to see when "spirit of bondage" is mentioned here that it's a small "s", and when Paul writes "Spirit of adoption" there's an emphasis on the large "S", as in Holy Spirit — who has all authority. Do you see that?

The phrase "Abba, Father" is an affectionate Aramaic term which means, "Daddy, Daddy" or "Papa." We are in a family, joined in union to the heart of the Father as sons and daughters. The Spirit bears witness and causes our identity to come alive in our spirit that we have become children of God. Not only children, but heirs of God with Jesus (v.16,17), whether they are biological or adopted, have the same benefits of provision and inheritance.

I love that word, "benefits." Psalm 103:2-5 says, *"Praise the Lord, my soul, and forget not all his benefits — who forgives all your sins and heals all your diseases, who redeems your life from the pit and crowns you with love and compassion, who satisfies your desires with good things so that your youth is renewed like the eagle's."*

No Slaves & No Orphans

Take your time to absorb these passages in your spirit and your soul that are being given in this chapter. They are transformational, and key to your identity and victory as a child of God. Our Father doesn't want us alienated, wandering in a orphan spirit and way of thinking. You are loved and cherished.

> *"But when the fullness of the time had come, God sent forth His Son, born of a woman, born under the law, to redeem those who were under the law, that we might receive the adoption as sons". "And because you are sons, God has sent forth the Spirit of His Son into your hearts, crying out, "Abba, Father!" Therefore you are no longer a slave but a son, and if a son, then an heir of God through Christ."*
> Galatians 4:4-7

When it comes to your personal identity with God, how do you perceive yourself? Be honest. Are you a stranger, a sinner saved by grace – doomed to always fail? Are you a slave or servant? Or are you a son or daughter? The only way to properly perceive yourself accurately is to agree with what your Heavenly Father has spoken over your life.

> *"Behold what manner of love the Father has bestowed on us, that we should be called children of God! Therefore the world does not know us, because it did not know Him. Beloved, now we are children of God; and it has not yet been revealed what we shall be, but we know that when He is revealed, we shall be like Him, for we shall see Him as He is."*
> 1 John 3:1-2

The word *repent* means, "to change your way of thinking; going one direction and changed to another." Repentance is a beautiful gift of God that brings us into change and transformation. Repentance is the changing agent of God's grace and gives us access into the heart of God and empowers us to see ourselves accurately. A large part of repentance is agreeing with God and His Word regarding Who He is and who we are in Him. This where our minds are renewed and transformed.

> *"To them God willed to make known what are the riches of the glory of this mystery among the Gentiles: which is Christ in you, the hope of glory."*
> Colossians 1:27

Is that epic? It's mind boggling that the dream of God was to live and dwell within us. What a dream! What a God! Christ is in you. This is a part of the metamorphosis that occurs through His Spirit and His Word.

> *"I beseech you therefore, brethren, by the mercies of God, that you present your bodies a living sacrifice, holy, acceptable to God, which is your reasonable service. And do not be conformed to this world, but be transformed by the renewing of your mind, that you may prove what is that good and acceptable and perfect will of God."*
> Romans 12:1&2

To "be conformed to the world" is to be lost as orphans — not knowing whom their Father is — disconnected, alone, abandoned, lost, wandering. You and I are called to be transformed, an awakening to this revelation that we are sons and daughters of the Living God. This changes everything. This is the real hope and beauty of life. Friend, you are not an orphan. You are a chosen, beloved, celebrated son and daughter in the kingdom with honor, privilege, benefits and inheritance. We are being transformed continually by the Holy Spirit as He reveals to us this unfolding mystery that we are in God and God is in us. We are one with God.

> *"And all of us, as with unveiled face, [because we] continued to behold [in the Word of God] as in a mirror the glory of the Lord, are constantly being transfigured into His very own image in ever- increasing splendor and from one degree of glory to another; [for this comes] from the Lord [Who is] the Spirit. "*
> 2 Corinthians 3:18 | Amplified Version

Before we move onward, I want to encourage you to look at the difference of living as a son verses living as a slave. Remember, God desires this revelation as sons and daughters to transform us. It would surely be enough if this revelation were only intended for just ourselves - for our personal victory and freedom. Transformation always begins in the heart and spirit of an individual. But as we move forward, we become awakened to a grander vision from our Father. Transformed sons and daughters will transform their cities, regions and nations. Take a moment to identify the belief of Sons and Daughters in the Kingdom vs. the perspective of Slaves and Orphans:

Sons and Daughters:
Believe and experience the unconditional love of the Father.
Experience Sonship as an heir, based on their position to the Father.
Rest in the security of their Father's provision.
Are still loved when they fall short.
Are stewards of what the Father entrusts to them.
Love their Dad's character.
Values are totally based on position as a Son and Daughter.
Experience Love.

Receive gracefully.
Recognize sins and have a repentant heart.
Live from the heart.
Believes they are loved.
Lives a godly Kingdom lifestyle defined by grace and redemption.
Live under God's authority.

Slaves & Orphans:
Believe they must perform to gain the Father's love.
Believe becoming an heir is tied to performance, not their position as children.
Believe provision is only through performance.
Believe they deserve judgment when they fail.
Believe they are entitled to a share of anything they do.
Resent their Dad's character.
Values are only based on what they do and how well they do it.
Love is earned.
Expect an entitlement.
Are self-righteous, prideful.
Live from legalism.
Believe they are defective, producing shame.
Have a worldly kingdom perspective defined by performance and posturing.
Reject God's authority.

We are a sons and a daughters, and because our identity as children of God has been firmly established, we are called and commissioned to make a global impact to whatever sphere of life that The Holy Spirit sets on fire within our souls. In the kingdom, sons and daughters live in a culture of revelation, prophecy, faith and supernatural activity. In my travels, I like to use Southwest Airlines. Southwest's slogan is: "You are now free to move about the country." I like to say, "You are now free to move about The Kingdom." Who knows the dreams that God has dreamed for you? I know you want to discover those dreams and live in those adventures.

Remember the epic prophecy from Joel that the Apostle Peter announced on the day of Pentecost as the Holy Spirit was being poured out? God says in the last days:

"I will pour out of My Spirit on all flesh; Your sons and your daughters shall prophesy, Your young men shall see visions, Your old men shall dream dreams. And on My menservants and on My maidservants I will pour out My Spirit in those days; And they shall prophesy." (Acts 2:17&18)

Let me say again, in the kingdom, sons and daughters live in a culture of revelation, prophecy, faith and supernatural activity.

Be Free & Be True At Your Core

Years ago, a prophetic friend spoke a life-giving word into my heart that has helped me navigate and walk in freedom when it comes to our identity and the call of God. He encouraged me not to be limited to one title and one function. He told me that I would wear many hats in life and never to be bothered by those who tried to put the limitations of titles and restrictions upon me, those that said I could only do this, or could only do that. He encouraged me to stay free and just function in freedom to what the Father was calling me to do in every season of life.

Some people are locked in a prison of the identity that other people have tried to create for them. It's so unfortunate. Regardless of the boxes and smallness that people try convince you of or peddle stories to others about you, you have to learn how to move in your own direction, following your heart and following the Holy Spirit. I've been told that I'm only a pastor. I've been told I'm only an evangelist. I've been told that I'm only a prophet or a revivalist. Truthfully, I'm satisfied with just being, Brian — a son of God. We are free to live and live boldly in who God has ordained for us to be as sons and daughters. There is great freedom in the kingdom for us all, to live creatively and express the nature of God.

You have to be faithful and true in your core to who you really are and who you are becoming, not what others say you can do or not do. You and I are not called to fulfill the vision that other people have for us. We are called to fulfill the vision and purpose that God has dreamed for us. God is a transforming God — an ever-increasing progressive God. He has plenty of hats that will look especially great on you.

Be free to evolve, change, retool and be who you are in your heart. Give yourself room and space to rediscover yourself as well.

There are giftings that are within that perhaps you haven't yet begun to tap into. The Holy Spirit longs to be your partner and bring those gifts to the forefront.

When I was young, all I wanted to do was be a rock 'n' roll drummer. I wanted to write epic songs that everyone would sing, shock people with massive drum solos and rock — loudly! Drumming was the only "skill" that I really excelled at and it set me apart. It was my gift. Everyone knew that I was "the drummer." Everyone in my hometown and region would talk about me being the drummer and that became my identity. I wasn't dreaming about leading people, writing books, being a prophetic voice, pioneering churches or pastoring people. I never saw myself as a leader. But God did, and His call is what actually set me apart.

Friends, you can wear the hat of ministry, you can wear the hat of marketplace and entrepreneurship. You can certainly impact more than one mountain. God can use you in government as sure as He can use you in the arts community. God can use you to rescue lives in a crack house and use you to be a voice in the White House. There are no limits in God. I want to encourage you, you need to be reminded that you can be all and become all that God sets on fire inside of your heart and your soul.

And when it comes to those with small thinking that look to handcuff you with limitations because they're aggravated by freedom, just remember something, they didn't want to see you blessed in the first place. Just tip your hats, smile humbly and be true.

Kingdom Friends — Champions

The gift of covenant friends is a treasure. I pray God gives you covenant friends who will burn with you and run passionately with you to ignite our world with His presence and power. The gifts and blessings that we pray for in life actually come to us in the packages of other people. Our job is to recognize and discern when those gifts are presented, so that we become the recipients of God's grace and goodness, in and through them. May you identity your band of brothers or your family of fire. Those that believe they just need God alone, they are terribly mistaken. You need God, that's obvious, but you also need kingdom friends in your life. I pray you find a company of burning hearts, just like yours.

You need friends in your life that are courageous, mature, spiritual and generous. You need true friends that can pray with you and for you, celebrate God's greatness in you and lift you. You need friends that are visionaries and forward thinkers. You don't need "friends" in your life that are jealous and envious of you, who can't pray for you because their mouths are filled with cynical and poverty mutterings. Those that are insecure and offended at you are satisfied with average and the status quo, and they decided long ago that they were good with living small.

You need champions in your life that are dreamers, faith walkers, builders, thinkers, pioneers, lovers and risk takers. You need friends who aren't carnal and lazy, and who aren't comfortable with celebrating good enough. You need friends of integrity who are not only there to complement your gifts, stay faithful in the storms of life, but who also challenge you to grow upward and move forward in God, and keep the standard lifted high. When enemies or giants appears, God calls out to the champions to arise and run forward to the battle. Chose friends whose boots march along side yours to the sound and rhythmic cadence of heaven's drum. Pursue quality life-giving friendships.

Discovering Purpose

You may be familiar with this passage from the book of Jeremiah. God says, *"For I know the plans I have for you," declares the Lord, "Plans to prosper you and not to harm you, plans to give you hope and a future."* The Nation of Israel was in exile and had been taken captive by Babylon for 70 years. You can imagine the defeat and hopelessness that clung to them. And yet in the midst of such great loss, God speaks through His prophet and tells them that He knows the plans, or the purpose, He has for them and it's a future of His blessing.

This is a beautiful promise of the intension of the heart of God towards all of us. God is a God of redemption. He's the one that liberates the captives. This word "plans" can also be properly translated "purpose." God knows the purpose and dream that He has designed for our lives. This purpose is to give us an anchored hope and a blessed future.

When I think about God knowing the purpose He has for me, it strengthens me to place all of my trust in Him. When we think in terms of "plan," so often we think that God has one plan for our lives and if we miss it, we could be doomed to a failing grade. When it comes to plans, this is not a passing or failing issue. God has thousands of plans that will bring you into the divine purpose that He dreamed over you before time existed. He told Jeremiah, that He knew him even before he was shaped and sculpted in his mother's womb in the creation process (see Jeremiah 1).

God knows the purpose (not just one plan) that He has over you and in that divine purpose you discover thousands of plans to carry you there. It's like driving in a car with a GPS. You set the GPS coordinates and it maps out the blueprint for you to arrive at your destination. Have you ever made a wrong turn with a GPS? If you have, you know that begins rerouting you immediately and starts talking, and talking, and talking to get you right back on the chosen path for your destination. It's simple, but revelatory. God knows your purpose. You may take some wrong turns here and there. (I'm not talking about sin or willful disobedience). You may get detoured or delayed here and there. There could even be seasons that you experience ambush or get sabotaged in the journey, but rest assured, The Holy Spirit is committed to Father's ultimate dream for your purpose. I dare you to be consumed with God and see how He will move to transform your life into the realm of the miraculous, the amazing and the extraordinary. Your purpose will continually be discovered in saying, "Yes", to the voice of Lord. This is a life long continual conversation with the Holy Spirit leading and guiding you in the calling.

Discovering Your Roar — The Prophetic Voice
"I wish you all spoke with tongues, but even more that you prophesied; for he who prophesies is greater than he who speaks with tongues, unless indeed he interprets, that the church may receive edification."
1 Corinthians 14:5

Have you ever heard the statement, "People don't care how much you know until they know how much you care?" I made this a core value many years ago, and I've tried to live by this throughout all my years pastoring and leading people. It's good to show people you care. It's good to express love through acts of kindness.

Stay with me here. For many of us, this little "live by" quote has done more harm than good. It's muzzled your voice, stifled your wisdom, shut your mouth and shut you down, while the people you care about are starving for a good word.

Yes, we need to show love. We desperately need the power of the Holy Spirit flowing through our hands in signs, wonders and miracles. But let's not forget that the Holy Spirit is also the voice of prophesy, words of wisdom, words of knowledge and gifts of faith that cry out to be expressed with words.

"Like apples of gold in settings of silver" (Prov. 25:11). That's how the Bible describes a word fitly spoken. Carefully chosen — not carelessly spoken — words can be precious, life-giving and live-saving to the people around you.

Many years ago, as a younger minister, I started realizing that people need words. They crave to hear something genuinely prophetic, from someone removed from the absolute closeness of their situation to speak life to them. Words release destiny. It could be the young man at the pizza joint downtown who's already lived a hard life. It could be your son or your daughter who's losing hope with a difficult marriage. The co-worker in the office next to you who needs to know God truly cares—and that He has the power to intervene in their desperate situation.

Unfortunately, many have lost the prophetic voice — their roar. Believers are reading their Bibles, listening to podcasts, attending church, mailing finances to missionaries, but the busyness of life and the proverbial phrase "People don't care how much you know until they know how much you care" has silenced many.

Life is busy. You're not going to be able to establish quality relationships with everybody and prove and affirm to them how much you care. But your consciousness and awareness of the abiding presence of the Holy Spirit within you will determine your ability to impart the life-giving words of heaven into any given situation.

Words That Release Destiny
(Taken from my book: "Unstoppable & Unquenchable Fire")

Jesus said, "It is the Spirit that gives life...the words that I speak to you, they are spirit, and they are life."
John 6:63

It had been a very long and challenging day. I was pastoring at the time, and thought it would be good to unwind and refresh, before heading home for the evening. I went down to Sarasota Bay Park to enjoy the ocean, some sunshine and some alone time with The Lord. As I was sitting in the grass, enjoying the breeze and a new book, a young couple got out of their car behind me and began to walk in my direction. As I looked up to see them passing by, acknowledging them, I noticed they were a very attractive couple, probably in their late 20's, walking hand in hand.

The Lord spoke to me so clearly, "Go tell them that they are to get married. Tell them that for all the trouble and adversity that they have experienced in their young lives, that God was going to give them the ultimate comeback and raise them up victoriously, and that they would have a ministry to young couples and families." I'm not a stranger to releasing prophetic words, but the whole "marriage" word shocked me! Its just prophecy 101 — You don't tell people whom they're supposed to marry. As a Pastor, I would be quick to correct or redirect anyone who gave that kind of a word at our church to a couple. I said, "Lord, for real? Do I have to tell them that?" His answer, "Yes, Son." He was overriding my prophecy 101 principle.

I went over and approached them as they were snuggling on a park bench, enjoying the ocean view. I politely introduced myself as a Pastor in Sarasota, I told them that as I was reading my book and had seen them walking into the park and that God spoke to me a beautiful word about their lives and their future.

The moment I told them that The Lord said that they were to be married, both of them began to tremble and burst into streaming tears. The young lady gasped. Their response was quite dramatic. I humbly gave the word and told them that the Lord loved them. The young man said, "Pastor, we are Christians and this is a true miracle for us. We attend a Slavic/Russian church here in Sarasota, and we have been on a fast for the last three days, praying for clarity, if indeed it was the Lord's will for us to get married."

They thanked me and said they would remember and treasure this day the rest of their lives. As I walked away and made my way back to my car, I sat watching this couple crying and holding one another. It was precious to behold. I sat and wept thanking the Holy Spirit for releasing such a special gift for them in this season of their journey.

There is nothing like partnering with The Lord to release His heart for others. Prophetic words release destiny. That is the roar of The Lion.

How do you find your prophetic roar? It all starts in your continual relationship with the Word of God and Holy Spirit. When the Lord is your delight and His word is your guide, you will burn with an unstoppable passion. When Jesus is your first love, you walk with the awareness that you are His hands, His love, His touch, His voice in this earth. As I said above, it is our consciousness to His abiding presence within that determines everything — our level of consecration, the miraculous, the prophetic. When you hear Him speak, believe it and act upon it. His life can flow effortlessly and words can heal. With a keen sensitivity to the Holy Spirit, you will learn the wisdom and the timing of God — the key to "a word fitly spoken."

"Pursue love, and desire spiritual gifts, but especially that you may prophesy. For he who speaks in a tongue does not speak to men but to God, for no one understands him; however, in the spirit he speaks mysteries. But he who prophesies speaks edification and exhortation and comfort to men."
1 Corinthians 14:1-4

What is prophecy? Prophecy at its most basic form is simply hearing God and speaking what you hear to men or women. Notice the foundation of the prophetic is love. Pursue love. The truth is, we'll never be effective in partnering with the Holy Spirit for others until you walk in love and feel the Lord's passion and carry His desires for others. Love is the foundation.

Look at what the Apostle Paul said above. Desire spiritual gifts. Don't miss that. Desire to prophesy. Desire to hear God and speak what He's communicating to you. What does prophecy do? In this passage above, Paul says it has three distinct characteristics. Prophecy edifies (which means to build up or bring structure), exhorts (life-giving, strengthening, encouragement) and brings comfort (bringing the awareness of God in their midst) to those who receive it. I pray that your heart would burn with desire to grow in the prophetic, so your roar is released to bring, hope, freedom, victory and life. What if there are words that the Holy Spirit wants you to hear and speak — to prophesy — bringing transformation to a life, a high school, a university, a city, a nation, a generation? I have good news for you sons and daughters. *"I will pour out of My Spirit on all flesh; Your sons and your daughters shall prophesy, Your young men shall see visions, Your old men shall dream dreams. And on My menservants and on My maidservants I will pour out My Spirit in those days; And they shall prophesy"* (Acts 2:17,18).

Let me say it one more time, in the kingdom, sons and daughters live in a culture of revelation, prophecy, faith and supernatural activity. It's time to ask, receive and roar.

Prophetic Justice

One night while ministering in a church in Indianapolis, we were hosting a prayer line for people with specific needs for healing. The altars were filled with several hundred individuals. After praying for a couple, I went back up on stage to make sure the ministry team wasn't missing any. I noticed an older lady was slowly making her way up to the front of the church and got into line. As I approached, I heard the Holy Spirit say the word, "Sonnet." That may not mean anything to you, but I knew what a sonnet was.

A sonnet is a particular poetic form or structure that originated in Italy, but became extremely popular through the poet and playwright William Shakespeare. A sonnet's main distinction is its pattern and structure that carries just 14 lines. The Holy Spirit highlighted 14 lines to me. I believe God has good things to say to people. He loves when we partner with Him to be a conduit of life in speaking His promises, desires and will to others. The Holy Spirit knows our language. He knows how to speak to us and draw from our database and life experiences. He is able to give us prophetic keys, enabling us to release life and healing to others.

I waited upon the Lord for a moment longer, and he directed my thoughts to Psalm 16:5&6, *"O Lord, You are the portion of my inheritance and my cup; You maintain my lot. The lines have fallen to me in pleasant places; Yes, I have a good inheritance."*

Lines in scripture give a picture of inheritance, posterity and generations. I believed The Lord was showing me something profound, but honestly it took some courage and faith (spelled R.I.S.K) to give this word. I committed myself and said to her, "You have 14 grandchildren and you are not to worry as the Lord shows me every one of them will be saved and brought into the kingdom. This is your inheritance and portion!"

The woman burst into tears and began to celebrate ecstatically, giving praises to the Lord. The Pastor asked me, "Do you know this woman and her family?" I didn't and was clearly nervous about what I had just shared. I think the Pastor was too. But the woman testified that she indeed had 14 grandchildren. They were the very reason she came forward to have prayer. She didn't realize that the prayer line was for healing. Frankly it didn't matter. God wanted to reward her years of prayer and intercession for her family. God has generations on his mind.

"But you are a chosen generation, a royal priesthood, a holy nation, His own special people, that you may proclaim the praises of Him who called you out of darkness into His marvelous light..."
1 Peter 2:9

BOLD AS LIONS

Chapter 8

LEADERSHIP
The Pathway To Triumph

"For as many as are led by the Spirit of God, they are the sons of God."
Romans 8:14

The Holy Spirit is the greatest leader on planet earth. God's anointed and called leaders are the most powerful force on the planet. Leaders have the opportunity, if they are wise, to shape the course of history and generations for good and for God's glory. What if your consecration and courage as a leader could shape the course of history? What if God is dreaming of using you and your partnerships with other kingdom leaders for the expansion of His dominion? He is.

When you study leadership, it's not long before you discover that some of the greatest leaders have emerged from the midst of extraordinary challenge, adversity, struggle, pain and conflict. My friend, Bishop Joseph Garlington says, "Leaders are not born, they're just cornered." Maybe that's why I've always loved Captain America since I was a boy. The key element of every notable leader is their uncommon commitment, passion and burning heart to overcome. Their lion-hearts will find the path to triumph.

It is no secret that the world is in a mess and upside down right now. White is Black. Black is White. Right is wrong and wrong is right. Evil is good and good is called evil. You could say that the world is in a famine of real leaders. Has there ever been a time when the contradictions were so glaring?

If you are presently a leader, or perhaps you feel called to a new level of leadership in some fashion, I pray this chapter is empowering and life-giving to your spirit and soul. I pray that that there will be a spiritual impartation and deposit from the Holy Spirit into your heart to soar and triumph. Your life, calling and purpose are so very important to the Lord. He believes in you.

The conflicts and epic battles of this hour are unprecedented and inescapable. The battlefields for spiritual, moral, political, educational, and governmental landscapes are ours for the taking. Leaders understand that we are called and appointed to bring God's wisdom, anointing and solutions into the trouble of this dark world. The kingdom of God was always meant to shape culture, never to retreat from it.

Anointed and courageous leaders will hear what others do not hear. They see what others do not see. They will say what others do not want to say. They will go where others are afraid to go. A courageous leader will not give people what they want but provide them with what they truly need. How does this happen? Their best friend and partner is the Holy Spirit who keeps them from the snare and bondage of the fear of man.

The world is in dire need of anointed and courageous leaders to step onto the local, national and global scenes. The Church desperately needs uncompromising leaders that are bold as lions. The governments of the nations and global structures are reeling with uncertainty. The answer lies within God's leaders. We need leaders that will carry heaven's heart and authority, know the agenda of the Father and refuse to compromise for the things of this earth.

Agents Of Change

"Now thanks be to God who always leads us in triumph in Christ, and through us diffuses the fragrance of His knowledge in every place."
2 Corinthians 2:14

We are in a very special season of time. The winds of change are blowing across the earth. We can, and we must, discover the pathway into the future now. The Spirit of God will prepare the way, and He's

LEADERSHIP

calling many to follow Him into a new anointing and a new strategic place of courageous leadership.

This is an hour of transcendence, a time of limitless possibilities. Perhaps, no generation of leaders, at every level of society and across the globe, has had such an opportunity to solve our greatest problems and bring the nations the unshakeable kingdom of God. You can stand up and be counted as a leader who will shine. You can establish a pathway of faith — a highway of holiness — forming a path to a better world for all the generations that follow.

As I have studied reformation, I have learned that at its core, reformation means to align, reconstitute, level and balance. To reform is to repair and restore what has been broken and corrupted. Reformation is divine order and alignment with The King's purpose, design and original intension.

A picture of divine alignment is found in the greek word, *katartizo*. This means to adjust and put something back into its appropriate position. The word is used in Matthew 4:21 concerning the disciples mending nets. In 1 Corinthians 1:10, it's referred to as repairing schisms or relational breaks. In Galatians 6:1, this word is used in restoring broken lives. The word is also used to describe the restoration of a dislocated joint or broken bone. My friend Dutch Sheets says, "Katartizo is God's special work as the Holy Chiropractor."

God is grooming and anointing leaders who will carry a divine *katartizo* shift to restore and mend cities, states and nations back to their God-appointed purpose and destiny.

Now is the time to ask for the pure wisdom that comes down from above (see James 3:17). We cannot attempt to solve the world's issues with a secular mindset. Our leadership must come from the fresh breath of the life-giving Word and Spirit of God. True leaders lead from the heart of loving the truth and serving the truth by sacrificial love and honor.

I believe the global prayer movement that has been freshly energized by the Spirit of God in the last decade will see a release of emerging leaders born out of burning prayer communities of intercessors, watchmen, gate keepers and five fold ministries.

"Those from among you shall build the old waste places; You shall raise up the foundations of many generations; and you shall be called the Repairer of

BOLD AS LIONS

> *the Breach, The Restorer of Streets to Dwell In."*
> Isaiah 58:12

> *"And they shall rebuild the old ruins, They shall raise up the former desolations, And they shall repair the ruined cities, The desolations of many generations."*
> Isaiah 61:4

Leaders are God's keys to the future. They will unlock the answers and solutions for societal transformation. Don't be so quick to gloss over the scriptures above. Anointed leaders will arise in this hour from among us. They have been uniquely trained and forged by the Spirit of God to rebuild, raise up, repair and restore the foundations.

Reformers are the restorers who reconstitute, level and set into alignment that which has been torn apart and desolated. They have been set apart and consecrated. They have refused to be conformed to the spirit of the age and God has anointed them with heavenly wisdom, innovation, creativity and authority to bring the increase of His government.

Down through history, God has raised up and positioned reformational leaders as the times demanded for the healing of breaches and broken places, to bring nations back into alignment with His heart. God has always worked through these consecrated vessels as they are His agents of change for human history.

The Spirit of God seeks men and women who are willing to stand up valiantly against the forces of darkness invading our society. Deep in the reformer's spirit is the standard that they cannot accept the status quo, business as usual and things as they are. They refuse to let the trends of the world around them shape and define them. They are non-conformists, and they refuse to play the games of their lukewarm generation. Reformers are not afraid to be the passionate and different ones. They have chosen the holy burnings of heaven's agenda.

The Holy Spirit & Leadership
> *"For as many as are led by the Spirit of God, they are the sons of God."*
> Romans 8:14

The greatest collaboration for releasing power and mobilizing

LEADERSHIP

leaders that can change the world is found in the Person of the Holy Spirit. Kingdom leaders are set apart and established in His grace and calling. They are those who are directed and led by the Spirit of God.

In the book of Acts, Luke begins with, *"Dear Theophilus, in the first volume of this book I wrote on everything that Jesus began to do and teach until the day he said good-bye to the apostles, the ones he had chosen through the Holy Spirit, and was taken up to heaven."* Notice that Jesus was guided by the Holy Spirit to select His leaders. All throughout the Book of Acts, we see this continued pattern. The presence of the Holy Spirit identified leaders that were chosen to serve and care for widows (Acts 6:3-6). The Holy Spirit identified and set apart Saul and Barnabas as two leaders commissioned to preach the Gospel in Salamis (Acts 13:2-5). The Holy Spirit chose and appointed leaders to shepherd the church. Acts 20:28 says, *"Keep watch over yourselves and all the flock of which the Holy Spirit has made you overseers. Be shepherds of the church of God, which he bought with his own blood."*

The Holy Spirit empowers leaders with supernatural boldness. In Acts chapter four, the text reveals that Peter, filled with the Holy Spirit, spoke to the leaders. Peter and John were empowered by the Spirit with courage and boldness to speak unapologetic truth to the influential leaders of their day. In Acts 4:13, we see that these leaders were baffled and perplexed. *"When they saw the courage of Peter and John and realized that they were unschooled, ordinary men, they were astonished and they took note that these men had been with Jesus."* This same profound boldness shined through Stephen in Acts chapter six. *"These men began to argue with Stephen, but they could not stand up against his wisdom or the Spirit by whom he spoke."*

The Holy Spirit will always compel leaders to leave their comfort zones far behind to break into new territories. The Apostle Paul was profoundly used by the Holy Spirit to preach the gospel and he too wasn't aloud to remain in a place of comfort. Acts 20:22-24 says, *"And now, compelled by the Spirit, I am going to Jerusalem, not knowing what will happen to me there. I only know that in every city the Holy Spirit warns me that prison and hardships are facing me. However, I consider my life worth nothing to me, if only I may finish the race and complete the task the Lord Jesus has given me – the task of testifying to the gospel of God's grace."*

The Holy Spirit's presence and influence in our day-to-day leadership must be activated through our sensitivity to His leadership and our courage to obey His voice. Without Him, we could attempt doing leadership solely out of our own wisdom and strength, which will amount to nothing. We must remember, it is the anointing of the Holy Spirit that destroys the yoke of bondage (Isaiah 10:27). He is our true source of power. God's purposes and desires become a reality in the earth when leaders make their partnership with the Holy Spirit.

All spiritual leadership and true visionaries draw from this secret — they abide in the One who is the Leader — The Lion King. It is not just a cliché, it's a profound truth, that the greatest spiritual leaders are the greatest followers of Jesus.

Revelation is the Key to Leadership.
"Let a man so consider us, as servants of Christ and stewards of the mysteries of God. Moreover it is required in stewards that one be found faithful."
1 Corinthians 4:1&2

Leaders are those who treasure what is sacred and they honor what is holy. Paul says that they steward the mysteries of the kingdom. They carry the revelation of the kingdom that liberates the earth and expands heaven's culture. It is required of all leaders to walk humbly as we represent The Lord, bearing the mystery of a God who far surpasses any human capacity to fully define Him. Leaders are ones that are found faithful. Paul wrote his spiritual son, Timothy, and instructed him to make sure that he entrusted the gospel to faithful men (2 Timothy 2:2).

Our revelation of Jesus determines our authority, leadership function, capacity and ability to impart the life-giving presence of God to all we serve and love. The very nature of a leader is that they are carriers of a divine vision and burden of the Lord in their spirit. Kingdom leaders carry the culture and values of The Lord. Transformational leaders will carry generational vision, burden and fire for future sons and daughters.

Generational Blessing & Legacy
This is taken from my first book:
"Unstoppable & Unquenchable Fire"

In this present move of God we are beginning to see the signs of generational impartation and the promise of kingdom legacy being expanded far and wide. Legacy is powerful; it's an endowment, a gift and commission — released with the hopeful expectation of increase from generation unto generation. Paul instructs his spiritual son Timothy, *"And the things that you have heard from me among many witnesses, commit these to faithful men who will be able to teach others also"* (2 Timothy 2:2).

There are those who are in training right now to become mighty spiritual fathers and mothers. Faithful sons and daughters become faithful fathers and mothers. Your allegiance must be fully unto The Lord, but your faithfulness to Him is also revealed in how you choose to serve and honor those He has brought into your life as fathers.

One of the greatest privileges that we have is in choosing whom we will follow, so choose wisely. Follow wisdom and character. Follow those who live in true humility and love. Do not be caught up or mesmorised in a leader's gifts and charisma. Watch their lives to see their consistent integrity. No leader is perfect or infallible. Look for the marks of a true father who will invest and speak truth into your life — the beautiful truth and the ugly truth. We need people in our lives who will do more than just comfort us in a crisis or compliment our strengths and gifts. We need fathers who will commit themselves to challenging us to grow and to change. This is necessary.

We need fathers who will lovingly rebuke us in the healthiest way. The beautiful words of affirmation and empowerment are needed. So too, are the words of correction (hard sayings) and discipline.

Fathers and Sons
Mothers and Daughters

You cannot be apostolic if you don't have a heart for sons and daughters. It's no secret that fathers today are abandoning their wives, children and responsibilities. It's a tragedy. Sadly, it's a picture of the spiritual condition of our world, as we see these same patterns of abandonment taking place in ministry. Presently, around 1500+ pastors quit the ministry each month. This is so alarming. Without a doubt, ministry is tough. After more than 23 years of full-time ministry, I understand the challenges and the enormous load of responsibility that comes with leadership and becoming a spiritual father.

BOLD AS LIONS

Fathers and mothers bring rich perspective, wise counsel and protection to one's relationship with God. Their training, instruction, wisdom, covering, accountability and transparent lives are to be treasured. Having spiritual fathers and mothers help protect and safeguard the path and vision for your lives. They empower your God-given destiny and dream, regardless of weather it's to be a minister, a baseball coach, an actor, an artist, a senator, or an entrepreneur.

Spiritual fathers provide a safe and nurturing environment to grow and also help us to identify spiritual gifts. Spiritual maturity is vital in all of our lives, and spiritual fathers will put an appropriate demand on us to grow from adolescence into adulthood. *"When I was a child, I spoke as a child, I understood as a child, I thought as a child; but when I became a man, I put away childish things"* (1 Corinthians 13:11). For many, they remain stuck in a perpetual place of immaturity, because they lack the nurture and sound admonition of seasoned fathers and mothers. Spiritual fathers model a standard of excellence and call forth that spirit of excellence in their sons and daughters.

Teachers instruct, but fathers love and build up. Teachers instruct but fathers impart. I am deeply grateful to the amazing fathers and mothers that the Lord has brought throughout my life, to help shape and develop me. I'm additionally thankful that they didn't ignore my mistakes but gracefully corrected me and pointed me forward. While so many leaders in our generation are waffling and wavering in a cesspool of social trends and compromise, I'm thankful for the fathers and leaders in my life who have kept burning faith, maintained integrity and remained faithful on the ancient path — the tried and true road. (see Jeremiah 6:16)

You need spiritual fathers and mothers in your life. It is imperative that you pray and seek to establish relationships (real kingdom connections) that will enhance and lift your spiritual trajectory and maturity. The passion of The Spirit is the return of apostolic fathers towards sons and daughters and sons and daughters toward fathers (see Malachi 4:6). Malachi's prophetic word is a beautiful picture of the generations from the youngest, to the most seasoned, working together to advance the kingdom of God.

To father the fire and perpetuate the kingdom's legacy, we must raise spiritual sons and daughters that have learned the secret of a saturated lifestyle in His Presence. Our aim must be to bring them to a place of character, where as mature sons and daughters, they carry the government of God. Only mature sons and daughters, who are discipled by godly fathers and mothers, will be able to rule with nobility in the high places of cultural influence.

We must create an atmosphere where it's the norm to linger before the Lord in prayer, and gaze upon His wonder and glory. You must father sons and daughters through example, so their first and greatest ministry is unto the Lord. It's not people first. It's Father first. Lead them to cultivate a sacred lifestyle of encounter in the riches of the Word and with The Holy Spirit, through prayer, worship and fasting. Empower them to be courageous and brave, living as a nonconformist to the spirit of the age (see Romans 12:2).

Invest time, revelation and life experiences into their development. Our greatest legacy is not what we leave *for* people, but what we leave *within* them. Invest. Live an uncompromising and consecrated life before them. Let our testimony be a standard, witnessing God's empowerment and grace to a surrendered life.

God must be represented by those who are not bound by time. A spiritual father and mother are a timeless people who understand that their sacrifices, obedience, honor, joy, and life contributions are going to impart into a generation that perhaps isn't even born yet. Ecclesiastes 3:11 says, *"He has made everything beautiful in its time. Also He has put eternity in their hearts, except that no one can find out the work that God does from beginning to end."* We must understand that the eternity which has been set in our hearts, will not be completely unfolded and revealed in our lifetime, but will find its fullness in generational legacy.

Dear Leaders, I want to encourage you to make a personal commitment to serve, build and foster relationships that will perpetuate the kingdom of God. Make it your aim to live and plan skillfully to invest and empower young men and women. We need each other, and we need mature and courageous leaders for the hour ahead of us. We are dependent upon one another.

Together we can overcome the independent, orphan spirit that has plagued the Body of Christ for far too long. Remember, there are those who are in training right now to become mighty spiritual fathers and mothers. Faithful sons and daughters become faithful fathers and mothers.

(In my book, "Unstoppable & Unquenchable Fire" I explore in great detail the power of generational blessing and shepherds after God's own heart — See Chapter four — Generations: Fathering The Fire.)

Kingdom Leaders
"Be watchful, stand firm in the faith, act like men, be strong. Let all that you do be done in love."
1 Corinthians 16: 13&14

A kingdom leader will exemplify and inspire a spirit of loyalty and honor. They live a life and set an example that others desire to follow. They will live a lifestyle of integrity and build a legacy of nobility. A real leader is not just a cheerleader for mere principles; it is their life that speaks and shines giving witness to the reality of the Lordship of Christ within.

Leaders have the ability to raise the bar and set the pace for those around them. Their hunger for God is contagious. Their passion for the Spirit will inspire and cause others to run for the prize. Their consecration and faithfulness will challenge shallowness and lukewarm hearts. Their compassion and care brings out the best in all that have eyes to see and ears to hear.

Leaders run with a heavenly vision in their obedience to the Spirit of God. They create vision for others, they articulate the vision, passionately own the vision, and help others learn to run with fire. That's why Jesus was the most epic leader to walk planet earth. He was unstoppable and unquenchable.

Leaders behave wisely. From time to time, you will have a mouth full of blood from biting down on your own tongue. Leaders keep their mouths shut even when they want to react or respond. There will be times when Wisdom says; "remain silent." Sometimes you lead by what you don't say, and your integrity will just have to bleed.

Leaders will create and establish an environment for developing a culture of lovers, worshipers, intercessors and dreamers. They give wings for others to soar higher and dream grander and go farther. Our goal should be to create a culture that brings forth lions and lionesses that are powerful and prophetic — not professionals. Leaders know that they have the ability and responsibility of raising mature sons and daughters. Their faith and transcendence can destroy the limitations and mindsets that have stifled generations.

Dear leader and dear friend, the pathway to triumph is found in a bold and courageous heart that will not tolerate compromise on any level. God is calling us to live holy, live wisely and live worthy of our calling. Our lions and lionesses are watching, and they need real leaders.

Whatever the Master says, do it. God is calling us to never retreat in the face of opposition and the present dangers of this age. The battles are fierce. It is time to live bold, think bold and be bold.

Wherever He Leads — Follow
"I will instruct you and teach you in the way you should go; I will guide you with My eye."
Psalm 32:8

One of my all-time favorite movies is "The Patriot" with Mel Gibson. Gibson's character, Benjamin Martin, is a family man that finds his world turned upside down in the midst of the Revolutionary War. The battle makes its way to his South Carolina doorstep reigning down bullets, cannons, bloodshed, fire and death — even on his own children.

Benjamin Martin and his oldest son, Gabriel, take up the cause to fight against the overwhelming British army. Their assignment is to find the right kind of courageous men and build a rebel militia to join the American troops.

There's a scene when a small village pastor leaves his pulpit and congregation behind to go and fight. During the Revolutionary War, there were many pastors and leaders that left their pulpits and congregation to join under George Washington's leadership; they were called the Black Robe Regiment. These patriot preachers engaged themselves fully to secure America's victory.

As the pastor prepares to leave with the rebel militia, he's stopped by his congregation as he's about to walk into the woods with the patriot soldiers. They ask, "Reverend, where are you going?" He turns to them soberly, removing his hat and says, "Sometimes a shepherd must stay and guard his flock, and at other times he must go and fight off the wolves."

BOLD AS LIONS

    I hear the roar of The Lion. He's saying, "Follow Me." Dear leader, whoever you are reading this book; wherever Jesus may lead you, I implore you — follow Him. Follow The Lion. It will be dangerous and glorious. Just follow Him. He is our Reward. The future belongs to the lion-hearts. The future belongs to the Righteous.

ABOUT BRIAN GIBBS

A Messenger. Founder of Light The Fire Ministries and Victory: A Church Of His Presence. Brian's ministry is marked with the diversity of igniting revival, pastoring, church planting, building leaders and reforming America. Many know him as a national and international revivalist. Those who know Brian personally know his greatest passions in life are his relationship with his Lord, his wife Bren, and their two children.

For more than 23 years, God has used the Gibbs to empower and mobilize the Body of Christ throughout the USA, Israel, Canada, Italy, Sweden, Pakistan, India and Central America. Their ministry is one marked with revival, uncommon favor, wonders and the fire of God. Brian & Bren reside with their two children and little Shih Tzu in Sarasota, Florida.

Light The Fire Ministries
Brian & Bren Gibbs
Igniting Revival | Equipping Leaders | Reforming America

VICTORY
A Church Of His Presence

Mailing
P.O. Box 51586
Sarasota, Florida 34232

Online
LightTheFireMinistries.org
VictoryFLA.com

Email
Brian@LightTheFireMinistries.org

Social Media
FaceBook.com
Brian.gibbs.90
Light.the.fire.ministries
Victory - A.Church.Of.His.Presence

Unstoppable & Unquenchable Fire
Published January, 2015
Author: Brian Gibbs
Foreword: Dutch Sheets

UNSTOPPABLE & UNQUENCHABLE FIRE is a burning message and passionate cry for personal revival, national awakening and generational reformation. This book was born out of encounters with the love of God and the fire of His holiness. It is no secret that we are in one of the most crucial times in human history here in America and the nations. I believe we are heading into a unprecedented shaking and troubles, but I also believe through the fire we will enter a Third Great Awakening - a move of God beyond anything we have ever conceptually imagined.

I believe this book is a must read for every Christian that longs to be an effective agent of change and transformation - for our times and the generations yet to come. This is a book of urgency and hope. Above all, its a call of when the burning heart of God ignites a life, invades our cities & recaptures a nation.

Thousands of readers have been ignited.

Order Today:
LightTheFireMinistries.org
Amazon.com (Available on Kindle)

Made in the USA
Columbia, SC
02 August 2020